flavors of VIRGINIA

Junior League of Northern Virginia

What Can I Bring Through the Seasons?

Copyright © 2017
by
Junior League of Northern Virginia
1420 Spring Hill Road
Suite 600
McLean, VA 22102

703-442-4163

Cookbook@jlnv.org

All rights reserved. No part of this publication
may be produced in any form without permission
in writing from the publisher.

ISBN: 978-0-692-89385-2

Manufactured in the United States of America

First Printing   2017

Copies of

Flavors of Virginia

are available by email or
online at www.jlnv.org

THE JUNIOR LEAGUE OF NORTHERN VIRGINIA

OUR MISSION:

The Junior League of Northern Virginia (JLNV) is an organization of women committed to promoting voluntarism, developing the potential of women, and improving the community through the effective action and leadership of trained volunteers. Its purpose is exclusively educational and charitable. Our vision is to empower women to be a driving force to improve our community.

ABOUT THE JLNV:

Nearly 400 women in the Northern Virginia area are members of the JLNV. Our members share a common desire to drive positive change in the community. In alignment with our mission, the League provides members with training and skills that will enrich their professional and personal lives. Training opportunities include leadership development seminars, workshops, project management opportunities and hands-on experience. Since 1958, the JLNV has provided more than 20,000 service hours toward JLNV programs and initiatives, 800 hours in leadership training, and more than $2.6 million in charitable grants to the community.

REACHING OUT STATEMENT:

The JLNV is committed to remaining a diverse and inclusive organization that is welcoming to all women with a passion for voluntarism, and to having a membership that reflects the rich diversity of the communities we serve. Our diversity enables us to more effectively address Northern Virginia's unique challenges and civic disparities spread across a large geographical area, and to partner with like-minded organizations that share our values. Additionally, the JLNV reaches out to women of all races, religions and national origins who demonstrate an interest in and commitment to voluntarism.

OUR IMPACT STATEMENT:

Childhood obesity has broad health consequences for children and families, and affects one in five children in Northern Virginia. The JLNV's focus area prepares children for success by addressing childhood obesity through the promotion of nutrition and physical activity education, which is proven to enrich health, well-being and academic outcomes. The JLNV is committed to reducing the number of children impacted by health disparities related to childhood obesity by empowering families to make healthier choices.

Learn more about the JLNV at www.JLNV.org.

Dear Friends of the Junior League of Northern Virginia,

While I am not a native Virginian, I'm proud to have claimed this state as my home and have settled here to raise my family. I've worked to establish strong roots and meaningful experiences in Northern Virginia, and my efforts have been rewarded with lasting friendships, a sense of belonging within the community, and a supportive network of like-minded women in the Junior League of Northern Virginia.

Life in Virginia also means having the benefit of experiencing the riches and changes that come with all four seasons: crisp, colorful autumns; chilly, snow-strewn winters; warm, inviting springs; and bright, sun-drenched summers. I particularly enjoy the seasonal produce that accompanies each season. While food and fellowship continues to be a hallmark of our League's history, more recently we've sought to address the growing concern of childhood obesity in Northern Virginia. Childhood obesity has direct links to poverty, a lack of access to fresh foods, and inadequate education on the topics of healthy eating and the importance of regular physical activity.

We know that eating local, fresh and in season is important to our health and well-being. To this end, *Flavors of Virginia* provides insight into produce that is table-ready during each season, and how to prepare these ingredients to make flavorful and nutritious meals. Proceeds from *Flavors of Virginia* directly benefit the Junior League of Northern Virginia's programming to improve the quality of life for children and low-income families in our region through education and empowering families to make healthy eating and lifestyle choices.

Louisa May Alcott wrote in her short story Mrs. Podgers' Teapot, "When women set their hearts on anything, it is a known fact that they seldom fail to accomplish it." I find this to be a fitting quote to describe our League's intrepid members. For 60 years, the Junior League of Northern Virginia has been committed to developing the potential of women to serve as change agents and civic leaders within their local communities. Year after year, our members serve tirelessly to move the needle on issues that continue to plague our most vulnerable citizens, and work steadfastly to open doors when all others have been closed.

We are grateful for the donors and supporters who continue to build the Junior League up. To those who have contributed to the "60 for 60 Giving Campaign" in honor of the Junior League of Northern Virginia's 60th anniversary, we say a special thank you. Thank you for your continued commitment and faith in the Junior League. We look forward to our next 60 years of service in the community, and as always, to more food and fellowship together. Happy cooking!

Yours in service,

Lori Ann
Lori Ann Terjesen, Ph.D.
2016-2017 President
Junior League of Northern Virginia

TABLE OF CONTENTS

FLAVORS OF VIRGINIA

WHAT CAN I BRING THROUGH THE SEASONS?

Flavors of Virginia: What Can I Bring Through the Seasons? is the second cookbook by the Junior League of Northern Virginia. The League's first book, *What Can I Bring?*, originally published in 1999, went through four printings, sold nearly 40,000 copies and raised more than $150,000 in support of the League's community activities.

Building on the success of *What Can I Bring?*, *Flavors of Virginia* highlights the bounty of fresh produce found seasonally in Northern Virginia. Local farmers' markets are full of fresh ingredients and opportunities to build healthy and delicious meals.

Recipes in this cookbook are showcased by season to feature the rainbow of fruits and vegetables available season-by-season and to make meal planning easier. This seasonal approach focuses on eating fresh, healthy foods and includes dietary notes on vegetarian (MEAT), gluten free and dairy-free recipes.

And while the book focuses on fresh fruits and vegetables and opportunities to lighten things up, there are also a few easy and delicious recipes you can make from your pantry when you are feeling indulgent.

We hope you'll enjoy the flavors of Virginia!

The recipes in this book have been tested for quality and edited for clarity and ease of preparation.

AUTUMN

As leaves are changing colors across Northern Virginia, so are weekend activities and the smells in the kitchen. Autumn is a season when farmers' markets are filled with every variety of apple, and hearty vegetables are making their way on to dinner plates.

In Northern Virginia, apple picking is in full force at the many farms and orchards in the area. When there are too many apple pies and apple crisps in the freezer, whip up some easy applesauce [page 13], baked French toast [page 16] or even a hearty autumn soup [page 28].

In addition to apple picking, pumpkins abound and can find their way into desserts and entrées alike. If the start of football season fills your weekends, whip up tailgate and game time treats everyone will love. Homemade dips are always a hit, or a batch of warm chili for a crowd to feast on together.

Celebrate the changing of the seasons with hearty home cooking celebrating the bounty of Northern Virginia.

What's Fresh In
AUTUMN?

Apples

Broccoli

Brussels Sprouts

Cauliflower

Cranberries

Grapes

Jalapeños

Mushrooms

Onions

Spinach

Pears

Potatoes

Squash
(Acorn, Butternut, Spaghetti, Delicata)

Sweet Potatoes

Turnips

AUTUMN RECIPES

SLOW COOKER APPLESAUCE

6 to 8 medium apples of the sweeter variety of apple (Gala, Crispin, Pink Lady)

4 to 6 cups water

1 teaspoon cinnamon (optional)

- Peel and core apples. Chop into small chunks (about 1-inch pieces).
- Place apples in slow cooker and cover with water. Use enough water to just cover the bottom of the slow cooker and apples.
- Cook for 4 to 6 hours on low, stirring occasionally. Mash for smoother applesauce or stir lightly for chunky applesauce. Stir in cinnamon if desired.
- Applesauce keeps well in an airtight container in the refrigerator for up to one week.

MAKES 3 TO 4 CUPS APPLESAUCE

Apple picking is a popular activity in Northern Virginia in the fall. When you get tired of apple French toast, apple pie and plain apples, this easy, healthy applesauce is a great way to use your orchard finds. Enjoy plain or stir into a bowl of hot oatmeal. You can also substitute applesauce for oil in many baking recipes to lighten up cakes or muffins.

PUMPKIN FRUIT DIP

1 cup pumpkin purée (not pumpkin pie filling)

1 cup plain, nonfat Greek yogurt

¼ cup honey or agave

1 teaspoon pumpkin pie spice

- Combine all ingredients in a medium bowl and mix until smooth. Serve with cut apples.

SERVES 4 TO 6

The Junior League of Northern Virginia Market Explorers program teaches children about eating fresh and locally. At the end of the program, explorers get to make a simple, healthy treat. This is great to make with kids, for kids as an after school snack, or as a fun treat to eat while watching a movie.

MUSHROOM BRUNCH CASSEROLE

6 slices cubed white bread

1 pound breakfast sausage
(hot or mild)

2 cups Cheddar cheese, shredded

4 eggs, beaten

8 ounces cremini mushrooms,
sliced

1 can (10 ounces) cream of
mushroom soup

1 small onion, chopped

2 tablespoons fresh parsley,
chopped

Salt and pepper to taste

- Preheat oven to 325°F.
- Lightly grease a 9 x 13-inch casserole dish.
- Place bread cubes in the bottom of the casserole dish.
- Brown sausage in medium saucepan and drain.
- In medium bowl, combine cooked sausage, cheese, eggs, mushrooms, cream of mushroom soup, and onion. Fold in chopped parsley and season with salt and pepper to taste.
- Pour egg and mushroom mixture over the bread cubes.
- Bake for 60 to 75 minutes, until casserole is firm.

SERVES 9 TO 12

NOTE: *Like other breakfast casseroles, this can be prepped the day before and refrigerated until ready to bake and serve. This recipe works with any variety of mushroom. For a more mild taste, try plain white mushrooms. Or add a teaspoon of truffle oil and a mixture of wild mushrooms for a more decadent dish.*

SUNDAY MORNING MUFFINS

2½ cups gluten-free flour (see below)

1 teaspoon baking powder

1 teaspoon baking soda

¼ teaspoon salt

½ teaspoon cinnamon

¼ cup maple syrup

⅓ cup coconut oil

⅓ cup unsweetened applesauce

1 egg

½ cup buttermilk

Mini chocolate chips to taste

Mini cinnamon chips to taste

Blueberries or dried cranberries to taste

Shredded coconut to taste

- Preheat oven to 350°F.
- Line a muffin pan with paper liners. Spray liners with nonstick cooking spray.
- In a large bowl, combine flour, baking powder, baking soda, salt and cinnamon. Mix well.
- In a medium bowl, mix together syrup, oil, applesauce, egg and buttermilk.
- Slowly stir the wet ingredients into the dry ingredients. Add flavorings (chips, coconut, dried fruit) to your taste. About 1 cup total of flavorings make very studded muffins.
- Fill muffin cups ¾ full with batter.
- Bake for 15 minutes.
- Remove from heat and let cool for 5 minutes in muffin tin, then remove from tins and cool all the way on cooling rack. Can be eaten warm or cold.

MAKES 12 MUFFINS

NOTE: *These muffins can be adapted to your taste, or whatever great fillings you have around. If you're looking for something sweet, try the chocolate and cinnamon chips, or if you prefer fruit flavors, try fresh or dried fruit and some shredded coconut or nuts.*

If you don't have gluten-free flour, you can also use regular flour. Any kind of gluten-free flour can work, or make your own by combining flours at these ratios.

HOMEMADE GLUTEN-FREE FLOUR

3 cups buckwheat

2 cups almond flour

2 cups potato starch

2 cups arrowroot flour

1 cup flaxseed meal

- In a large bowl, stir all ingredients together until well mixed. Store flour in an airtight container.

MAKES 10 CUPS GLUTEN-FREE FLOUR

BAKED APPLE FRENCH TOAST 

1 cup light brown sugar

1 stick butter

2 tablespoons light corn syrup or maple syrup

3 to 4 large apples (Honeycrisp, Empire, Gala, or Golden Delicious), thinly sliced

1 loaf challah bread, slightly stale

5 medium eggs

1½ cups milk

1 teaspoon vanilla

- Lightly grease 9 x 13-inch casserole dish.
- In a small saucepan, bring brown sugar, butter, and syrup to simmer on stove until thick.
- Pour mixture into casserole dish and spread evenly.
- Layer sliced apples over the syrup mixture.
- Slice challah bread into ¾-inch thick slices. Lay sliced bread over apples.
- In a medium mixing bowl, beat together eggs, milk, and vanilla.
- Pour evenly over bread.
- Cover and refrigerate 5 to 6 hours or overnight.
- Preheat oven to 350°F.
- Bake uncovered for 40 to 45 minutes.

SERVES 9 TO 12

PUMPKIN SPICE MUFFINS

1 box (18 ounces) spice cake mix
1 can (15 ounces) pumpkin purée

9 ounces cinnamon chips (optional)

- Preheat oven to 375°F.
- Line 18 muffin cups with paper liners.
- In a large bowl, mix spice cake mix, pumpkin purée, and cinnamon chips together until cake mix is completely moistened.
- Spoon batter into prepared muffin cups to about ⅔ full.
- Bake in preheated oven for 25 to 30 minutes, or until a toothpick inserted into the center comes out clean. Cool in the pan for 10 minutes before removing to cool completely on a wire rack.

MAKES 18 MUFFINS

NOTE: *These muffins are so easy and quick to make. They are great to whip up if you have last-minute guests arriving. Not only do they taste great, but they make your house smell amazing!*

HOT BUFFALO CHICKEN DIP 

8 ounces cream cheese, softened

½ cup buffalo hot sauce

¾ cup mozzarella cheese, shredded

½ cup plain, nonfat Greek yogurt

2 tablespoons ranch dressing mix

3 cups chicken, cooked and shredded

- Preheat oven to 350°F.
- Combine cream cheese, buffalo sauce, mozzarella, Greek yogurt, and ranch dressing in a medium mixing bowl until well-combined.
- Pour mixture evenly into an 8 x 8-inch baking dish.
- Bake uncovered for 20 to 30 minutes until heated through.
- Serve with tortilla chips, carrots, and celery.

SERVES 15 TO 20

This is a favorite for football game watch parties and tailgates. It's easy to make ahead and bake before serving (you can even cheat and use the microwave). Want to lighten it up? Use part-skim mozzarella cheese and reduced-fat cream cheese. If you don't have shredded chicken handy you can use canned chicken or leftover rotisserie chicken.

CARAMELIZED ONION DIP 

2 tablespoons olive oil

1 tablespoon butter

2 large onions, peeled and thinly sliced

Kosher salt and freshly ground black pepper

4 ounces cream cheese, room temperature

½ cup sour cream

½ cup mayonnaise

Fresh chives (optional)

- On the stove over medium heat, add olive oil and butter to a large skillet.
- When the butter has melted, add onions and season with salt and pepper. Cook for 20 to 30 minutes, stirring occasionally to ensure the onions do not burn. The onions should be caramelized and take on a deep golden brown color.
- While the onions are cooking, prepare the base of the onion dip in a large bowl. Beat the cream cheese on low speed until just smooth and free of lumps.
- Mix in the sour cream and mayonnaise to the cream cheese base.
- Fold the warm onions and any liquids from the pan into the dip base, and adjust salt and pepper to taste.
- Cover and refrigerate for at least 2 hours or up to 2 days to allow flavors to marry.
- Before serving, bring to room temperature and garnish with chives.
- Serve with vegetable crudité, chips, or crackers.

SERVES 8 TO 10

NOTE: *Want to lighten it up? Substitute 1 cup nonfat, plain Greek yogurt for the sour cream and mayonnaise. Add 1 tablespoon balsamic vinegar to give the dip added dimension and flavor.*

BAKED CHICKEN WINGS

2 dozen chicken wings
¼ cup peanut oil
   (can use vegetable oil)
1 teaspoon salt
1 cup flour

Wing or barbeque sauce
Carrot sticks, for serving
Celery sticks, for serving
Blue cheese or ranch dressing,
   for serving

- Preheat oven to 425°F.
- Line a sheet pan with parchment paper.
- Toss chicken wings in a bowl to coat with oil. Lightly sprinkle with salt.
- Dredge chicken wings in flour, tapping to remove excess. Lay wings in an even layer on lined sheet pan.
- Bake for 20 minutes, flip chicken wings over and bake for another 20 minutes or until wings are golden brown.
- Toss wings in your favorite sauce and serve with dressing, carrots, and celery.

MAKES 24 WINGS

NOTE: *Chicken wings are a popular football watching food, but are usually fried and heavy. This lightened up baked chicken recipe is so delicious your friends won't know the difference. Try setting up a chicken wing bar with an assortment of different wing sauces for guests to choose from.*

APPLE CHEDDAR QUESADILLAS 

2 teaspoons butter

2 teaspoons brown sugar

1 teaspoon cinnamon

1 large apple, peeled, cored, and thinly sliced

½ cup sharp Cheddar cheese, grated

4 large whole wheat tortillas

- In a skillet over medium-high heat melt butter. Stir in brown sugar and cinnamon.
- Add apple slices and sauté until soft.
- Spread grated cheese evenly on two tortillas.
- Spoon half of the apple mixture on top of cheese and top with remaining two tortillas.
- One at a time, place quesadillas back in the skillet (no need to rinse it) and cook on each side until crispy and cheese is melted (1 to 2 minutes per side).
- Allow to cool slightly, cut into quarters and serve.

MAKES TWO WHOLE QUESADILLAS

This is another kid-friendly Market Explorer recipe. It is a great way to get kids to eat apples in something they already love: tortillas and cheese. (This is also a great grown-up twist on the quesadilla and works great as a party appetizer, too.)

LENTIL SALAD 

½ **teaspoon ground turmeric**

½ **teaspoon ground coriander**

¼ **teaspoon ground red pepper**

¼ **teaspoon ground cloves**

¼ **teaspoon ground nutmeg**

¼ **teaspoon ground cinnamon**

½ **teaspoon ground mace**

1 **teaspoon dry mustard**

1 **teaspoon ground cumin**

1 **teaspoon salt**

1 **teaspoon pepper**

½ **cup red wine vinegar**

2 **tablespoons sugar**

½ **cup canola or corn oil**

1 **pound dried lentils**

1 **cup currants**

½ **cup capers**

1¼ **cups purple onion, chopped**

- Whisk together first 14 ingredients.
- Boil lentils in water for 5 to 6 minutes or until tender.
- Rinse and drain well.
- Combine lentils and dressing in a large bowl; marinate overnight.
- Add currants, capers, and onion to salad; marinate at least 2 hours.

SERVES 8 TO 10

We've added a few favorites from our first cookbook, and here is the first. Autumn is still fairly warm in Northern Virginia and this cold salad with a bit of nutmeg and cinnamon is the perfect way to accommodate the changing season, but lingering weather.

BAKED PINEAPPLE STUFFING

1 cup sugar

8 tablespoons (1 stick) butter

4 large eggs

1 can (20 ounces) crushed pineapple, drained

1 bag (15 ounces) potato bread rolls or burger buns, slightly stale

- Preheat oven to 350°F.
- Cut and cube stale potato rolls.
- Cream together sugar and butter with a hand mixer. Beat in eggs until combined.
- Stir in pineapple. Fold in cubed rolls.
- Lightly grease a 9 x 13-inch baking dish.
- Pour mixture into dish and bake for 30 to 45 minutes until golden brown on top.

SERVES 12 TO 15

NOTE: *Stuffing pairs great with ham or pork tenderloin.*

BAKED MACARONI AND CHEESE 

½ **pound dry macaroni**
1 **teaspoon butter**
1 **large egg, beaten**

1 **teaspoon salt**
1 **cup milk**
3 **cups sharp Cheddar cheese, grated**

- Preheat oven to 350°F.
- Grease an 8 x 8-inch casserole dish.
- Cook macaroni per package instructions in boiling water. Drain throughly.
- In large bowl, stir butter and egg into macaroni. Stir in salt and milk.
- Mix in 2½ cups grated cheese, leaving enough to sprinkle on top.
- Pour into prepared casserole dish. Top with remaining ½ cup cheese.
- Bake for 45 minutes or until top is crusty and golden brown.

SERVES 4 AS AN ENTRÉE

Baked macaroni and cheese is not only a Southern staple, but for many is a family tradition. This is a cherished side dish for holiday dinners, or to eat as a meal on special occasions. This also works great with a hearty, gluten-free noodle like rotini.

PUMPKIN MAC AND CHEESE

1 pound dry penne pasta

1 container (15 ounces) part skim ricotta cheese

1 can (15 ounces) pumpkin purée

¾ cup plain, nonfat Greek yogurt

2 eggs

1 teaspoon salt

1 teaspoon ground black pepper

½ teaspoon ground nutmeg

½ teaspoon garlic powder

1½ cups Parmesan cheese, grated

¼ cup fresh sage leaves, chopped

- Preheat oven to 375°F.

- Spray a 9 x 13-inch baking dish with nonstick spray.

- Cook pasta according to package instructions, reducing cooking time by 1 minute so pasta is al dente. Drain pasta and set aside.

- While pasta is cooking, mix together ricotta, pumpkin, yogurt, and eggs in a large bowl. Stir in salt, pepper, nutmeg, garlic powder, and ¾ cup grated Parmesan cheese.

- Fold cooked pasta into the cheese and pumpkin mixture.

- Pour mixture into prepared baking dish. Top with remaining ¾ cup Parmesan cheese and chopped sage.

- Bake uncovered for 35 to 40 minutes until golden and bubbly.

SERVES 6

NOTE: *This baked pumpkin macaroni and cheese works great as an entrée or side dish. Serve as an entrée with a light kale salad, or as a side dish with baked or rotisserie chicken.*

SWEET POTATO CASSEROLE 

6 large sweet potatoes
1 can (14 ounces) sweetened condensed milk
½ cup butter

1 teaspoon vanilla
½ teaspoon salt
2 large eggs, beaten well

TOPPING

½ cup brown sugar
⅓ cup flour

1 cup pecans, finely chopped
½ cup butter, melted

- Preheat oven to 350°F.
- Wash, peel and cube sweet potatoes. In a large pot of boiling water, cook potatoes until tender.
- While still warm, drain and mash sweet potatoes in a large mixing bowl.
- Add milk, butter, vanilla, salt, and beaten egg to mashed sweet potatoes.
- Using an electric mixer, cream mixture until smooth.
- Place mixture in a deep baking dish.

TOPPING

- In a small bowl, mix brown sugar, flour, pecans and melted butter together.
- Spread evenly over potato mixture.
- Bake for 30 minutes or until firm on top.

SERVES 8 TO 10

NOTE: *When you think of sweet potato casserole, you probably imagine the marshmallow-covered version. This is a sophisticated, marshmallow-free alternative that will impress friends and family at the Thanksgiving table. Best of all, you can make it the day before and reheat to save room in your oven.*

CORN AND RICE CASSEROLE

1 box (8 ounces) yellow rice

4 tablespoons (½ stick) butter

1 can (10 ounces) cream of celery soup

2 cups Mexican cheese, shredded

2 cans (15.25 ounces) whole kernel corn, drained (or use corn cut from 3 ears of corn)

- Preheat oven to 350°F.
- Prepare rice according to package instructions.
- Remove rice from heat. Add butter to rice, stirring until melted.
- Transfer butter and rice to a large heat proof bowl.
- Add cream of celery soup, 1 cup cheese, and corn. Mix together until combined.
- Pour mixture into lightly greased 8 x 8-inch baking dish. Top with remaining 1 cup cheese.
- Bake uncovered for 20 to 30 minutes, until bubbly.

SERVES 6 TO 8

NOTE: *This is a popular dish even for those who don't usually like corn. A great side during the holidays, this dish can also make an appearance in the summer using fresh corn. If you want leftovers, you might want to double the recipe for this crowd-pleaser.*

BUTTERNUT SQUASH AND APPLE SOUP 

4 cups low-sodium vegetable broth

16 ounces butternut squash, peeled and cubed

1 sweet onion, diced

1 large apple, peeled and diced

1 garlic clove, minced

1 tablespoon fresh sage, chopped

Salt and pepper to taste

- Combine broth, squash, onion, apple, and garlic in a large stock pot. Bring to a boil.
- Reduce heat to medium, cover, and let simmer for 15 to 20 minutes until squash is tender.
- Remove from heat. Stir in sage. Season with salt and pepper to taste.
- Using an immersion blender, purée soup until smooth. (If you don't have an immersion blender, transfer in batches to a blender and purée until smooth.)

SERVES 6 TO 8

NOTE: *If you want to add dairy, stir in 4 to 8 ounces of herbed goat cheese to make an even creamier and tangier soup.*

SPICY INDIAN CHICKPEAS (CHANA MASALA) 

- 1 pound fresh tomatoes with the stems removed or 1 can (14 ounces) crushed tomatoes
- 1 small yellow onion, peeled and quartered
- 2 garlic cloves
- 2 teaspoons ginger, peeled and grated
- 1 jalapeño pepper, roughly chopped
- 1 tablespoon vegetable oil
- 2 teaspoons cumin seeds
- 2 teaspoons paprika
- 1 teaspoon each tumeric, ground cumin, ground coriander, ground cinnamon, and garam masala (see note)
- ⅛ teaspoon cayenne pepper (optional)
- Salt to taste
- 2 cans (15 ounces) chickpeas, drained and rinsed
- ½ cup water
- 2 tablespoons lemon juice
- Cooked basmati rice, for serving

- Blend tomatoes, onions, garlic, ginger, and jalapeño in a food processor or blender until finely chopped, but not completely puréed.

- Heat oil in a large skillet over medium heat, add the cumin seeds and cook until fragrant, for about 1 minute. Stir in remaining spices and cook for 30 seconds. Add the tomato-onion mixture and cook for 5 to 7 minutes over medium-high heat.

- Add the chickpeas and water, and cook for 15 to 20 more minutes until the onions are thoroughly cooked. Add salt and lemon juice to taste.

- Serve over rice.

SERVES 4

NOTE: *You can add spinach to this dish for more iron, but may also want to increase the amount of spice. In place of the spice blend, you can replace with 1 ½ tablespoons chana masala spice mix. Whipping this up in the summer? Serve chilled chana masala mixed with rice as a cold salad.*

CAULIFLOWER STEAKS IN AGRODOLCE 

STEAKS

1 large head cauliflower

2 tablespoons olive oil

AGRODOLCE SAUCE

½ cup fresh mint, washed, dried, and finely chopped

½ cup dried currants, plumped in hot water for 5 to 10 minutes and drained

½ cup pine nuts, toasted

4 tablespoons red wine vinegar

½ cup olive oil

2 garlic cloves, minced

2 tablespoons capers, drained

2 teaspoons honey

STEAKS

- Preheat oven to 400°F.
- Cut cauliflower into four 1-inch thick steaks (through the core).
- On a rimmed baking sheet, brush cauliflower steaks with 2 tablespoons olive oil, coating both sides. Roast for 15 minutes. Flip steaks over, and cook for another 15 to 20 minutes, until cooked through and browned on both sides.

AGRODOLCE SAUCE

- Combine remaining ingredients in a medium bowl, stirring until well-combined.
- Serve cauliflower steaks immediately from oven, spooning sauce over the steaks.

SERVES 4

Agrodolce means sweet and sour in Italian, and is a very popular flavor in Italian cooking. This sauce is also excellent served on roasted Brussels sprouts and firm fish like halibut or salmon.

MEXICAN LASAGNA

1 can (14 ounces) red enchilada sauce, divided

3 cups Monterey Jack cheese, shredded

12 corn tortillas (6-inch), cut in half

3 cups chicken, pork or beef (leftover rotisserie chicken or cooked ground beef work well), cooked and shredded

1½ cups frozen or fresh corn or 10 ounces canned corn, drained

1 cup fat-free sour cream

- Preheat oven to 350°F.
- Spray a 9 x 13-inch baking dish with nonstick spray.
- Reserve ½ cup enchilada sauce and 1 cup cheese for topping.
- Spread ⅓ remaining enchilada sauce in the dish. Cover with a layer of tortillas.
- Top with ⅓ meat, ⅓ remaining cheese, ⅓ corn and ⅓ cup sour cream.
- Add another layer of tortillas and another ⅓ meat, cheese, corn, sour cream and enchilada sauce.
- Repeat again. Top with remaining tortillas, and reserved ½ cup enchilada sauce.
- Cover and bake 35 to 40 minutes.
- Uncover and top with reserved 1 cup cheese and return to oven for 5 more minutes until cheese is melted.

SERVES 6 TO 8

BANDOW'S BURRITOS

1 pound ground beef

1 tablespoon taco seasoning

**1 chipotle pepper in adobo sauce
(remove seeds and quarter)**

2 cups fat-free sour cream

1 can (15 ounces) corn

1 can (15 ounces) black beans

8 large flour tortillas

1 jar (15 ounces) salsa

**2 cups cheese (Cheddar or
Mexican blend), shredded**

- Preheat oven to 350°F.
- Spray a 9 x 13-inch baking dish with nonstick cooking spray.
- Over medium heat, brown ground beef with taco seasoning. Drain and set aside.
- Stir chipotle pepper in sour cream and let it sit for 10 minutes. Remove the pepper and set aside (or leave some mixed in for extra spicy burritos).
- In a large bowl, mix beef, corn, beans and sour cream.
- Put ¾ cup filling in each tortilla in the baking dish. Roll up and top with salsa and shredded cheese.
- Bake uncovered for 30 minutes.

SERVES 4 TO 5

NOTE: *This can be prepared ahead of time. Add the salsa and cheese just before baking.*

TURKEY CHILI

1 tablespoon olive oil

1 large yellow onion, chopped

5 garlic cloves, minced

2 pounds 99 percent fat-free ground turkey

2 cans (15 ounces) kidney beans

1 can (15 ounces) black beans

1 orange bell pepper, chopped

1 red bell pepper, chopped

1 yellow pepper, chopped

1 can (28 ounces) crushed tomatoes

1 can (15 ounces) petite diced tomatoes

3 tablespoons tomato paste

1 tablespoon brown sugar

3 tablespoons chili powder

½ teaspoon cayenne pepper

Salt and pepper to taste

- In a large pan, heat olive oil on stovetop.
- Sauté onion and garlic until onion is translucent, then remove onions and garlic and set aside in large slow cooker.
- Add ground turkey to pan, cooking until brown. Drain excess fat.
- Add meat to onions and garlic in slow cooker. Stir in beans, peppers, tomatoes, tomato paste, and brown sugar.
- Stir in chili powder and cayenne pepper. Add salt and pepper to taste. Mix well.
- Cook on low heat in slow cooker for 8 hours.

SERVES 10 TO 12

NOTE: *This is a great slow cooker recipe that can be made ahead of time. Top with cheese and sour cream or separate into individual portions and freeze for another day. This recipe is great for a cold fall day.*

VODKA SHRIMP RIGATONI

1 pound uncooked rigatoni

1 pound raw shrimp, peeled and cut horizontally into two pieces each

2 tablespoons olive oil

1 large yellow onion, peeled and thinly sliced

1 can (28 ounces) crushed tomatoes

½ teaspoon crushed red pepper flakes

¼ cup vodka

½ cup heavy cream

15 to 20 fresh basil leaves, cut into thin strips

Kosher salt and freshly ground pepper

- Salt a pot of water generously and bring to a rolling boil.

- Add the pasta and cook for 11 to 12 minutes, stirring occasionally. Add the shrimp and cook until they turn pink, about 1 minute. Check the rigatoni for doneness, reserve about 1 cup pasta water, and then drain the pasta and shrimp. Set aside.

- Heat the oil in a large saucepan, add the onions and cook on medium-high heat until slightly translucent, about 5 to 7 minutes. Reduce heat to medium, add the tomatoes and crushed red pepper flakes and simmer for 5 minutes. Add vodka and heavy cream, and simmer for an additional 5 minutes. Season with salt and pepper to taste.

- Add pasta and shrimp to the saucepan. Stir in ¾ basil. Toss all ingredients until thoroughly coated with the sauce, adding some of the pasta water if more liquid is needed. Garnish with additional fresh basil, if desired, and serve hot.

SERVES 6 TO 8

NOTE: *The key to making perfect pasta is project management and a lot of salt. Always put your water on to boil before you start to make your sauce, and don't hold back on salting the water. If you put the water on the stove first, you can easily get this meal on the table within 30 minutes. Most pasta sauces are meant to taste fresh, so be sure not to overcook your sauce: 15 to 17 minutes of cooking time for the sauce should do it.*

PORK POT PIE WITH SWEET POTATO BISCUIT CRUST

PORK

1 tablespoon olive oil

Salt and pepper

4 to 5 garlic cloves

4 pound pork shoulder/butt, fat trimmed

3 medium onions, sliced

3 Granny Smith apples, peeled, cored, and wedged

4 cups apple cider

1 cup beef stock

1 sprig fresh thyme

SWEET POTATO BISCUIT CRUST

¾ cup puréed sweet potato

½ cup buttermilk

6 tablespoons very cold butter, grated

1½ cups flour

1 tablespoon baking powder

1½ teaspoons salt

PORK

- Heat oil in a large pot over high heat. Salt and pepper pork generously and put some sliced garlic cloves in the pork. Sear all sides of the pork. Remove pork from pot and set aside.

- Add onions to pot and cook until tender, scraping the bottom of the pan (about 5 to 6 minutes).

- Add pork back to pot. Add apples, apple cider, beef stock, and thyme. Bring to a boil.

- Lower heat and simmer covered for 3 hours.

- Remove from pot and chop or shred like you are making sloppy joes.

SWEET POTATO BISCUIT CRUST

- Whisk together the sweet potato purée and buttermilk. In a separate bowl, toss the grated butter with the flour, baking powder and salt. Stir the flour mixture into the sweet potato mixture just to combine.

PUTTING IT TOGETHER

- Put pork mixture in the bottom of a standard pie plate. Drop the sweet potato dough by 2 tablespoons evenly on top of the pork. Make a couple of slits in the top.

- Bake at 400°F for at least 40 minutes. Cover with foil when there are about 10 minutes remaining to prevent from getting too brown.

SERVES 6

NOTE: *If you have leftover pork, use the next day for pulled pork sandwiches or sloppy joes.*

MAPLE APPLE AND PEAR PIE 

3 cups Fuji apples, peeled and thinly sliced

3 cups Anjou pears, peeled and thinly sliced

2½ tablespoons cornstarch

Dash of salt

⅔ cup pure maple syrup

2 refrigerated roll-out pie crusts

1 tablespoon unsalted butter, cut into small pieces

2 tablespoons sugar

- In a large bowl, toss together apples, pears, cornstarch, and salt. Drizzle maple syrup over mixture and gently stir to combine.

- Place one pie crust in a 9-inch pie plate and let edges hang over sides.

- Drain as much liquid as you can from fruit mixture. Spoon mixture into crust and dot with butter.

- Cover pie with the second crust. Trim edges to 1-inch overhang, fold over and pinch crusts together.

- Sprinkle sugar over crust. Cut several slits or designs in the crust to allow steam to escape.

- Refrigerate pie for at least 15 minutes before baking.

- Place oven rack in lower ⅓ of oven. Preheat oven to 375°F.

- Bake chilled pie at 375°F for 15 minutes.

- Reduce heat to 350°F and bake additional 45 to 60 minutes or until crust is golden brown and fruit is tender. (Cover edges of crust with foil during last 15 minutes of baking if they are browning too quickly.)

- Cool for at least 30 minutes before serving.

SERVES 8

NOTE: *Want to add creative flair to your double crust pie? Instead of covering your pie with a rolled crust, use your favorite seasonal cookie cutters to cut the crust into shapes. Lay the shapes over the filling, ensuring there is enough coverage with small gaps for steam. Seal the pieces together with a quick brush of beaten egg white. Try leaf or pumpkin shapes for an extra fall look.*

ICE CREAM "POTATO" BAR

1 quart ice cream
½ cup regular cocoa powder
**¼ cup red cocoa powder
(optional)**

⅓ cup chocolate chips
Whipped cream
Chocolate syrup
Bacon pieces

- Leave the ice cream out at room temperature for 10 minutes to soften.

- Place regular cocoa powder in two separate bowls.

- Scoop tennis-sized balls of ice cream and place them in the bowls of cocoa powder. Roll the ice cream balls in cocoa powder to coat. Roll and press ice cream into potato-like shapes. If using the red cocoa powder, it can be used to make the ice cream look like red-skinned potatoes.

- Press chocolate chips into the "potatoes" for eyes. Place all potatoes on a small pâté or cookie sheet (can stack since they are coated in cocoa powder). Return to the freezer until ready to serve.

- When ready to serve, put the ice cream potatoes out with whipped cream, chocolate syrup, and bacon for topping.

SERVES 6 TO 8 (OR MORE IF SETTING UP FOR KIDS)

NOTE: *This is a great, kid-friendly recipe that makes plain ice cream a little more fun. Try setting this up for a kid's birthday party or as a great afternoon treat.*

MONIKA'S DOUBLE CHOCOLATE CUPCAKES 

2 ounces semisweet chocolate chips

1 cup hot-brewed coffee

2 cups sugar

2 cups all-purpose flour

1 cup unsweetened cocoa powder

1 teaspoon baking soda

½ teaspoon baking powder

¾ teaspoon salt

2 large eggs

½ cup vegetable oil

1 cup buttermilk, well-shaken

1 teaspoon vanilla

CHOCOLATE BUTTERCREAM

3 sticks (12 ounces) unsalted butter at room temperature

4½ cups powdered sugar

6 tablespoons half-and-half or whole milk

6 ounces semisweet chocolate, melted and cooled

2 tablespoons vanilla

- Preheat oven to 350°F.

- Line two 12 cup cupcake/muffin pans with cupcake paper liners.

- In a medium ovenproof bowl, combine chocolate chips with hot coffee. Let mixture stand, stirring occasionally, until chocolate melts and mixture is smooth.

- Into a large bowl, sift together sugar, flour, cocoa powder, baking soda, baking powder, and salt.

- In another large bowl, beat eggs with an electric mixer until thickened slightly and lemon colored (about 3 minutes with a standing mixer or 5 minutes with a hand-held mixer). Slowly add oil, buttermilk, vanilla, and melted chocolate mixture to eggs, beating until completely combined. Add sugar mixture and beat on medium speed until just combined.

- Fill each cupcake liner ⅔ full.

- Bake 20 to 25 minutes until a toothpick inserted comes out clean. Let cupcakes cool slightly then remove from pan and let cool completely before frosting.

- While the cupcakes cool, prepare the frosting.

CHOCOLATE BUTTERCREAM

- Using a whisk attachment, whip butter until creamy (for about 30 seconds).

- Add ¾ cup powdered sugar and 1 tablespoon half-and-half at a time to the butter mixture. Whip as you go, alternating until you've used all the powdered sugar and half-and-half. Whip until fully incorporated.

- Check to make sure the melted chocolate is fully cooled, then add to the buttercream mixture. Whip until fully incorporated. Add vanilla and whip for an additional 3 to 5 minutes until buttercream is light and fluffy.

- Use a pastry bag and decorating tip (any large round or star tip) to pipe buttercream onto each cupcake. Cupcakes are best the same day, but can be made ahead of time if necessary. Covered cupcakes should last 2 to 3 days.

MAKES ABOUT 5 CUPS FROSTING AND 24 CUPCAKES

Monika's Cupcakes are a staple at many Junior League of Northern Virginia events, including the annual Placement Palooza where members select their committee placements. The coffee in the batter gives the cake a deep chocolate flavor while the buttermilk creates the perfect cake. This frosting is almost mousse-like, but this is the perfect chocolate cake base for any frosting.

CHOCOLATE CHIP PUMPKIN COOKIES 

½ cup butter

1 cup sugar

1 egg

1 teaspoon vanilla

7½ ounces pumpkin purée
(½ of 15 ounce can)

2 cups flour

1 teaspoon baking soda

1 teaspoon baking powder

½ teaspoon salt

1 teaspoon ground cinnamon

1 pinch nutmeg

½ cup semisweet chocolate chips

- Preheat the oven to 375°F.
- Grease 2 cookie sheets with nonstick cooking spray.
- In a large bowl, cream the butter and sugar until smooth with an electric mixer.
- Beat in the egg. Mix in the vanilla and pumpkin until well-blended.
- In a separate bowl, stir together the flour, baking soda, baking powder, salt, cinnamon, and nutmeg.
- Stir dry mixture into pumpkin mixture. Fold in chocolate chips.
- Drop by tablespoons (or your preferred size) onto the prepared cookie sheets.
- Bake for 12 to 15 minutes in the preheated oven, until edges begin to brown.
- Allow to cool for a few minutes on the baking sheets before moving to wire racks to cool completely.

MAKES 24 COOKIES

APPLE NOODLE KUGEL 

1 package (8 ounces) egg noodles

2 tablespoons butter, melted

4 eggs (can add up to 8 to make it fluffier)

1 cup sugar

¼ cup golden raisins

¼ cup dark raisins

2 tablespoons ground cinnamon

½ teaspoon vanilla

4 Red Delicious apples, sliced into long thin wedges

Cinnamon to taste

- Preheat oven to 350°F.

- Grease an 11 x 7-inch baking dish with nonstick cooking spray.

- Cook noodles according to package instructions and drain. Stir melted butter into cooked noodles.

- Slowly stir eggs into the bowl of noodles.

- Add sugar, raisins, cinnamon, and vanilla into noodle mixture until mixed well.

- Spread half of the noodle mixture into baking dish.

- Spread apples on top of the noodles. Add the remaining noodles to the top until all apples are covered. Sprinkle with cinnamon to taste.

- Bake uncovered for 45 minutes or until firm.

- For an extra firm dish, cut dish into squares and continue to cook until it reaches your desired consistency.

- Serve as a side dish or dessert.

SERVES 6 TO 8

GRAMMA'S PUMPKIN BREAD 

3½ cups all-purpose flour
2 teaspoons baking soda
1½ teaspoons salt
1 teaspoon cinnamon
1 teaspoon nutmeg
3 cups sugar

4 eggs, beaten
1 cup vegetable oil
⅔ cup water
1 can (15 ounces) pumpkin purée
1 cup pecans, chopped (optional)

- Preheat oven to 350°F.
- Lightly grease and flour two 9-inch loaf pans.
- Sift together in a large bowl the flour, baking soda, salt, cinnamon, nutmeg, and sugar.
- Add beaten eggs, oil, water, and pumpkin purée to dry mix.
- Beat with electric mixer until smooth.
- Fold in chopped pecans, if using.
- Divide equally into prepared bread pans.
- Bake for 1 hour in preheated oven until toothpick inserted in bread comes out clean.

MAKES 2 LOAVES

NOTE: *This is a great, easy pumpkin bread recipe that freezes well. Serve plain or with a side of whipped cream cheese for an extra treat.*

NOTES

WINTER

WINTER

As temperatures get colder, Northern Virginia braces for one or two heavy snowstorms each winter. The holiday season means decorations all over town, and baked goodies pop up as seasonal staples at markets and in our kitchens.

It's a season to highlight the rich flavors of root vegetables. Turning them into soups or stews [pages 70-73], they simmer on stoves and in slow cookers. Meanwhile, easy treats like spiced pecans [page 58], sweet and sticky cinnamon breads [page 55], and decadent cookies [pages 74-75] get whipped up on the weekend and brought to school and work to celebrate the season.

For many, winter also means visitors and family. Old-fashioned casseroles [page 64] with a fresh twist can feed a crowd and make cooking ahead of time a breeze. Highlight fresh meats with a Bolognese or a bourguignon sure to fuel a hungry family.

What's Fresh In
WINTER?

Beets

Brussels Sprouts

Cabbage

Carrots

Celery

Grapefruit

Greens
(Kale, Swiss Chard, Spinach)

Leeks

Mushrooms

Onions

Oranges

Parsnips

Pears

Potatoes

Pumpkins

Sweet Potatoes

Turnips

WINTER RECIPES

SMALL GROUP SPINACH QUICHE

1 package (10 ounces) frozen chopped spinach
4 eggs
1 cup Greek yogurt
1 cup small curd cottage cheese
½ cup Parmesan, grated
¼ cup whole wheat flour
2 cups Mexican cheese, shredded
1 frozen pie crust shell (9-inch)

- Preheat oven to 400°F.
- Place the spinach in a microwave-safe container and cook on high for 2½ minutes to defrost.
- Allow spinach to cool. Wrap the spinach in a towel and squeeze to remove excess liquid. Pulverize spinach in food processor.
- In a medium bowl, combine eggs, Greek yogurt, cottage cheese, Parmesan, and flour. Whisk together until the mixture is smooth, for about 1 minute.
- Slowly stir in spinach and Mexican cheese until well-combined.
- Fill the frozen pie crust shell with the spinach mixture and smooth out the top.
- Coat a piece of tin foil with cooking spray. Cover the pie tightly and bake in preheated oven for 45 minutes.
- Remove foil and bake an additional 10 to 15 minutes or until top is golden brown and filling is set.
- Allow to cool slightly prior to cutting.

SERVES 6

The Junior League of Northern Virginia alternates all League meetings with small groups, allowing members to get to know one another better. This is a favorite dish for a small group brunch during cooler months.

SLOW COOKER OATMEAL

1½ cups unsweetened almond milk

2½ cups water, divided

2 large apples, peeled and cut into ½-inch cubes (about 3 cups)

1 cup uncooked steel-cut oats

2 tablespoons brown sugar

¼ teaspoon ground cinnamon

¼ teaspoon salt

Maple syrup, to serve

Chopped walnuts, to serve

- In a saucepan over medium-high heat, bring almond milk and 1½ cups water to a boil, stirring frequently.
- Spray a slow cooker with cooking spray.
- Put hot milk mixture, apples, oats, sugar, cinnamon, and salt in slow cooker. Stir well.
- Cover and cook on low for 7 hours or until oats are tender.
- Spoon oatmeal into bowls and drizzle with maple syrup and walnuts.

SERVES 8

NOTE: *This keeps well in the fridge for up to a week. Make on Sunday and serve in individual containers for a quick grab-and-go oatmeal breakfast during the week.*

CORN FLAKE BREAKFAST CASSEROLE

2 pound bag shredded hash brown potatoes, thawed

1 teaspoon salt

¼ teaspoon pepper

1 large onion, diced

1 can (10.5 ounces) cream of chicken soup

1 pint sour cream

2 cups sharp Cheddar cheese, shredded

½ cup butter, melted

2 cups corn flakes, crushed

- Preheat oven to 350°F.
- Prepare a 9 x 13-inch casserole dish with nonstick cooking spray.
- In a large bowl, mix hash browns, salt, pepper, onion, cream of chicken soup, sour cream, and cheese.
- In a separate bowl, mix melted butter and crushed corn flakes.
- Pour hash brown mixture into prepared casserole dish. Top with crushed corn flakes.
- Bake uncovered for 45 to 50 minutes.

SERVES 8 TO 10

NOTE: *If you prefer hash browns over eggs, this is an egg-free breakfast casserole. It freezes well, so if you are serving a smaller crowd, divide into two smaller casserole dishes to save one for another day.*

SAUSAGE-HASH BROWN CASSEROLE

1 pound mild ground pork sausage

1 pound hot ground pork sausage

1 package (30 ounces) frozen hash browns

1½ teaspoons salt, divided

½ teaspoon pepper

1 cup Cheddar cheese, shredded

6 large eggs

2 cups milk

- Preheat oven to 350°F.

- Cook sausage in a large skillet over medium-high heat, stirring until sausage crumbles and is no longer pink. Drain the fat well.

- Prepare hash browns according to package directions, adding ½ teaspoon salt and pepper.

- Stir together hash browns, sausage, and cheese. Pour into a lightly greased 9 x 13-inch baking dish.

- Whisk together eggs, milk, and remaining 1 teaspoon salt. Pour evenly over potato mixture. Bake 35 to 40 minutes.

SERVES 8 TO 12

NOTE: *Want to lighten it up? Try using spicy turkey sausage in place of pork. Choose a reduced-fat cheese, skim milk, and replace eggs with 1½ cups of liquid egg substitute. Like other breakfast casseroles, this is easy to make ahead and put in the oven in the morning. And leftovers are great reheated.*

CINNAMON BREAD

1 cup milk, plus a few tablespoons, reserved
¼ cup vegetable shortening
1 packet yeast
¼ cup warm water
2 teaspoons salt

1 egg, slightly beaten
3½ cups flour
1½ cups sugar
¼ cup ground cinnamon
2 to 3 tablespoons butter, melted

- Preheat oven to 350°F.
- In a small saucepan, heat 1 cup milk to almost boiling (starting to form small bubbles). Let cool.
- In a separate small saucepan or microwave, melt vegetable shortening. Let cool.
- Pour yeast packet into warm water and let sit 10 minutes to activate.
- Mix heated milk, vegetable shortening, activated yeast, salt, egg, and flour in a large bowl. Mix well by hand or with an electric mixer. Once well-mixed, empty the dough onto the counter and knead for a few minutes.
- Grease a medium- to large-sized bowl.
- Place the dough in the greased bowl and let sit in a warm spot, covered by a kitchen towel, until the dough doubles in size.
- Punch the dough (it will deflate). Turn the dough out onto the countertop and let sit for 10 minutes.
- In a small bowl, mix sugar and cinnamon.
- Using a rolling pin, roll the dough into a rectangular shape (18 to 24-inches long).
- Brush the top of the dough with the few tablespoons of milk.
- Sprinkle the cinnamon sugar mixture over the length of the dough, leaving ½-inch bare on each side.
- From one short end of the dough, start rolling the dough into a "tube" shape.
- Grease a 9-inch bread pan. Place the dough, seam side down, into the bread pan.
- Brush the top of the dough with melted butter. Sprinkle with additional cinnamon if desired.
- Let the bread pan sit in a warm spot, covered by a kitchen towel, until the dough rises to 1-inch above the top of the pan.
- Bake for 50 minutes.

MAKES 1 LOAF

NOTE: *This bread is a big hit on holiday mornings. Serve hot and sliced or make ahead and toast slices on a baking sheet in the oven before serving with butter and jam. If you prefer even more cinnamon flavor, use ½ cup cinnamon.*

BABA GANOUSH EGGPLANT DIP 

2 medium eggplants

2 tablespoons extra virgin olive oil, divided

2 to 3 garlic cloves, minced

¼ cup tahini

¼ cup fresh lemon juice

Salt to taste

- Preheat over to 350°F.
- Slice eggplants into 1-inch thick rounds. Brush both sides with 1 tablespoon olive oil. Spread on rimmed baking sheet.
- Roast eggplants for 45 minutes to 1 hour, flipping half way through cooking.
- Let eggplants cool to room temperature. Remove eggplant skin (it should peel off easily).
- Cut rounds into smaller pieces and place in food processor. (If your food processor isn't large enough, work in half batches.) Add garlic, tahini, lemon juice, and olive oil to food processor.
- Pulse until combined (this dip should be chunky).
- Serve at room temperature with pita chips or crudité.

MAKES APPROXIMATELY 2 TO 3 CUPS

NOTE: *This is a great alternative to hummus and a different way to highlight the flavors of beautiful farmers market eggplants.*

HAM ROLLUPS

1 pound thick cut deli ham, sliced
4 ounces cream cheese, softened

1 bunch green onions, ends trimmed

- Take a slice of deli ham and lay if flat. Apply a thin coating of cream cheese to one side.

- Lay a green onion at one end and trim so it's the same length as the ham.

- Roll up the ham into a roll with the cream cheese inside and the green onion in the middle. Slice into 1-inch pieces and pile them on your serving plate.

MAKES APPROXIMATELY 50 ROLLUPS

NOTE: *This is a very simple recipe. Easy and kid-friendly to assemble, this appetizer is a protein-packed alternative to chips and dip.*

SASSY SAUSAGE DIP

1 package (16 ounces) hot or spicy sausage
1 can (12 to 14 ounces) of diced salsa-style tomatoes

12 to 16 ounces cream cheese
Picante sauce to taste

- Brown sausage in a skillet over medium heat, stirring until it crumbles and is no longer pink; drain well.

- Combine sausage, tomatoes, and cream cheese in a microwave-safe bowl.

- Microwave at HIGH in four minute intervals, stirring after each interval until thoroughly heated.

- Stir in picante sauce to taste.

- Serve with chips.

SERVES A CROWD

NOTE: *This is another favorite from our previous cookbook. This dip is a perfect side to bring to any football get-together.*

HOLIDAY SPICED PECANS

1 egg white, slightly beaten

2 tablespoons cold water

½ cup sugar

¼ heaping teaspoon ground cloves

¼ heaping teaspoon allspice

¼ heaping teaspoon cinnamon

½ teaspoon salt

4 cups pecans, halved

- Preheat oven to 250°F.
- Combine egg white, water, sugar, spices, and salt, mixing well. Set aside for 15 minutes.
- Stir in pecans and mix.
- Spread evenly on two greased cookie sheets (or lay out parchment paper and lightly spray with cooking spray). Bake for 1 hour.
- Immediately loosen pecans from sheets with a spatula. Store in an airtight container.

NOTE: *These are great to have out at a holiday party and also make great, easy gifts. Put spiced nuts in individual mason jars and tie with a bow for teachers, neighbors, coworkers, or friends.*

HOLIDAY MEATBALLS

MEATBALLS

1 pound ground beef

¾ cup plain breadcrumbs

2 tablespoons white onion, minced

1 tablespoon ketchup

1 teaspoon horseradish or to taste

4 dashes hot sauce

½ teaspoon cumin

½ teaspoon paprika

¼ teaspoon onion powder

2 eggs

1 tablespoon Parmesan cheese, grated

Salt and pepper to taste

SAUCE

1 cup ketchup

1 cup chili sauce

¼ cup cider vinegar

½ cup brown sugar

4 dashes hot sauce

½ teaspoon dry mustard

½ teaspoon paprika

Salt and pepper to taste

MEATBALLS

- Preheat oven to 400°F.
- Combine all ingredients for meatballs in a large bowl. Form meatballs and place on rimmed baking sheet.
- Bake about 20 minutes until fully cooked.

SAUCE

- On the stove in a medium saucepan, combine all ingredients for sauce. Stir and simmer for 20 to 30 minutes.
- In a serving dish, pour sauce over meatballs. Toss to coat and serve.

MAKES ABOUT 18 MEDIUM SIZED MEATBALLS

NOTE: *Make smaller meatballs to serve as an appetizer using toothpicks or serve for dinner over cooked egg noodles or rice.*

SOUTHERN GREEN BEAN CASSEROLE 

1 pound green beans, fresh or frozen

¼ cup water

4 tablespoons butter, divided

2 tablespoons flour

3 tablespoons white onion, grated

½ teaspoon salt

½ teaspoon ground pepper

1½ teaspoons sugar

12 ounces sour cream

2 cups Swiss cheese, shredded

1 cup corn flakes

½ cup Cheddar cheese, shredded

- Preheat oven to 350°F.
- Spray a 9 x 13-inch baking dish with nonstick cooking spray.
- Steam green beans in large microwave safe bowl with ¼ cup water. Cover tightly with plastic wrap. Microwave on high for 5 to 7 minutes.
- Over medium heat, melt 2 tablespoons of butter in a large saucepan. Stir in the flour and cook for 3 to 4 minutes, stirring constantly until thick.
- Stir in onion, salt, pepper, and sugar. Cook for 3 to 4 minutes, until soft.
- Whisk in sour cream.
- Stir in Swiss cheese.
- Add cooked green beans to the sauce, stirring to coat. Pour green beans into prepared baking dish.
- In a medium bowl, combine the corn flakes with remaining 2 tablespoons melted butter.
- Top green bean mixture with the Cheddar cheese and then corn flakes.
- Bake for 30 minutes or until bubbly.

SERVES 10 TO 12

SOUTHERN LADY SHRIMP AND GRITS

**1 cup quick cooking grits
(not instant, can use white
or corn grits)**

1 tablespoon butter

12 ounces andouille sausage

1 tablespoon flour

2 tablespoons cold coffee

¾ cup water

**1 pound raw shrimp, shelled and
deveined**

- Prepare grits according to package instructions. When cooked, stir in butter and set aside.

- Cut sausage into ¼-inch rounds and then quarter each disc.

- In a large frying pan, brown the sausage until cooked.

- While the sausage is browning, in a small bowl combine flour and cold coffee, mixing until incorporated.

- Stir the coffee mixture into the cooked sausage and slowly add water. Add the shrimp, cooking until pink (about 3 minutes).

- Spoon shrimp and sausage mixture into the grits and serve.

SERVES 6

NOTE: *Want to lighten it up? The sausage gives this recipe great flavor, but you can substitute chicken sausage and add ½ teaspoon Cajun seasoning and a few dashes of hot sauce to replace the sausage and keep the flavor. This dish is a crowd-pleaser for brunch or dinner.*

EASY WEEKNIGHT CHICKEN POT PIE

1 teaspoon olive oil

1 bag (16 ounces) frozen mixed vegetables (or use 1 pound mixture of fresh diced carrots, onions, and peas)

1 teaspoon Italian seasoning

Salt and pepper to taste

¾ pound boneless, skinless chicken breasts, cooked and cubed

1 can (10 ounces) cream of chicken soup

1 cup low-sodium chicken broth

1 can (8 ounces) crescent rolls

- Preheat oven to 350°F.
- In a large skillet, heat olive oil and sauté mixed vegetables. Stir in Italian seasoning, salt, and pepper. Cook vegetables until tender.
- Add cooked chicken and cream of chicken soup. Slowly add chicken broth until mixture is a creamy consistency.
- Line the bottom of a 9 x 13-inch casserole dish with unrolled crescent rolls. Use 3 to 4 rolls until covered.
- Top evenly with chicken filling. Top mixture with remaining crescent rolls until covered.
- Bake 20 minutes or until crescent rolls are browned.

SERVES 8

NOTE: *This recipe is a weeknight crowd-pleaser: chicken pot pie without having to roll out dough and assemble individual pies. Individual servings can also be cooled and frozen in individual bags to be reheated later. This recipe is also a great use for leftover rotisserie chicken.*

CHICKEN STROGANOFF

8 ounces egg noodles

1 pound boneless, skinless chicken breasts, cubed

½ teaspoon garlic powder

1 teaspoon olive oil

1 package (¾ ounce) dry Italian-style salad dressing mix

8 ounces cream cheese

1 can (10 ounces) low-sodium cream of mushroom soup

- Prepare noodles according to package instructions. Drain and set aside.
- Season cubed chicken with garlic powder.
- In a large skillet over medium-high heat, cook chicken in olive oil (about 5 to 6 minutes).
- In a separate saucepan over medium heat, combine salad dressing mix, cream cheese, and soup. Cook until warmed through and stir in chicken.
- Pour mixture over egg noodles.

SERVES 4

CHICKEN CASSEROLE

2 cups chicken, cooked
1 can (10 ounces) reduced-fat
 cream of mushroom soup
½ cup plain, nonfat Greek yogurt
1 cup celery, chopped

⅓ cup onion, chopped
2 tablespoons butter, melted
2½ cups cornbread stuffing mix
 (or stale cubed corn bread)

- Preheat oven to 350°F.
- Combine chicken, soup, yogurt, celery, and onion in a medium bowl. Mix well. Pour into 8 x 8-inch casserole dish.
- In a separate bowl, toss melted butter with cornbread. Spread evenly on top of chicken mixture.
- Bake 30 minutes.

SERVES 4

NOTE: *This is an easy weeknight dinner recipe that is always a crowd-pleaser. If you don't have cooked chicken handy, boil a couple of chicken breasts in chicken broth until cooked, and then shred. Serve with a side of green beans or a salad.*

ITALIAN SPAGHETTI SAUCE WITH BEEF

2 tablespoons olive oil, divided
4 garlic cloves, minced
1 green bell pepper, chopped
1 small white onion, chopped
2 carrots, grated
1 pound fresh mushrooms
2 pounds lean ground beef
1 large can (28 ounces) crushed tomatoes

2 cans (6 ounces) tomato paste
2 tablespoons fresh parsley, minced
1 teaspoon oregano
1 tablespoon salt
1 teaspoon pepper
¾ cup red wine

- Heat 1 tablespoon oil to medium-high heat in a heavy stock pot and cook garlic, green pepper, onions, and carrots until tender (about 5 to 7 minutes).

- In a large skillet, sauté mushrooms in 1 tablespoon oil for about 6 minutes. Add mushrooms to other cooked vegetables.

- Use the empty mushroom skillet to brown the beef, breaking it up as you cook. Drain any excess fat and liquid.

- Add ground beef to vegetable mixture. Stir in tomatoes, tomato paste, parsley, oregano, salt, and pepper. Finally, add the wine.

- Reduce heat and simmer for about 2 hours until flavors combine. Serve over fresh pasta.

SERVES 10 TO 12

NOTE: *Even longtime fans of jarred spaghetti sauce say this one is worth the time. It has a great depth of flavor and puts fresh vegetables to use. It freezes well so you can keep it handy for nights when you need a quick meal.*

BUFFALO BOLOGNESE

¼ cup olive oil

½ cup carrots, shredded

½ large red onion, diced

1 pound ground bison (can also use extra lean ground beef)

1 tablespoon oregano

1 tablespoon dry basil

2 tablespoons tomato paste

4 garlic cloves, minced

1 cup red wine

1 tablespoon Worcestershire sauce

1 can (28 ounces) whole plum tomatoes

½ cup milk

Salt and pepper to taste

Red pepper flakes to taste

Parmesan cheese, for serving

- Heat oil over medium heat in a large pot or Dutch oven. Cook carrots and onions for 3 to 5 minutes until tender.

- Add ground bison to the pot, cooking for a few minutes until brown. Stir in oregano and basil.

- Stir in tomato paste and garlic and cook for a few minutes more. Stir in red wine, Worcestershire, and canned tomatoes.

- Slowly add milk, salt and pepper, and as much red pepper flake as you can handle.

- Reduce heat to low, cover, and simmer at least 30 minutes. Can simmer for up to 3 hours.

- Serve with a thick cut pasta – tagliatelle, fettuccine, and penne all work well. Top with Parmesan cheese and serve.

SERVES 6 TO 8

NOTE: *Ground bison is leaner than chicken and now available in most grocery stores. Using it for this Bolognese gives the sauce a rich, meaty flavor without all the fat. This sauce can be made quickly or simmer for a few hours. Whip it up for dinner and let it continue cooking until you set it aside to cool and freeze or save for leftovers.*

SMOKY BUTTERNUT SQUASH CHILI 

1 pound ground beef
2 garlic cloves, minced
Salt and pepper to taste
1 small sweet onion, diced
1 pound butternut squash, cubed
1 green bell pepper, diced
1 can (15 ounces) tomato sauce
1 can (15 ounces) diced tomatoes
1 can (15 ounces) vegetarian baked beans

1 can (15 ounces) black beans, drained and rinsed
1 cup canned whole corn, drained
3 tablespoons chili powder
2 tablespoons brown sugar
2 teaspoons smoked paprika
¾ teaspoon salt
½ teaspoon garlic powder
½ teaspoon cumin
½ cup water

- In a large pot over medium heat, brown ground beef. Add garlic and season with salt and pepper while cooking. Break up meat into small pieces as you cook.

- Add onion and cook until translucent (1 to 2 minutes).

- Stir in butternut squash, bell pepper, tomato sauce, tomatoes, beans, corn, seasonings, and water.

- Simmer covered for 45 minutes stirring occasionally.

SERVES 6 TO 8

The addition of butternut squash bulks up the chili and gives it a slightly sweet flavor. Consider topping with shredded cheese, sour cream or Greek yogurt, chopped green onions, or tortilla chips. This chili is also great served with a side of cornbread.

SUPER SIMPLE CHILI

1 teaspoon olive oil

2 garlic cloves, minced

1 large onion, diced

1 large red or green bell pepper, diced

1 pound ground beef

1 can (14 ounces) diced tomatoes

1 can (14 ounces) red kidney beans, with liquid

3 tablespoons tomato paste

Salt

Black pepper

1 tablespoon smoked paprika

2 tablespoons chili powder

1 teaspoon cayenne pepper

- In a large pot over medium-high heat, heat oil and sauté garlic, onion, and bell pepper until soft (3 to 5 minutes).
- Reduce heat to medium, add the ground beef and brown.
- Stir in tomatoes, beans with liquid, and tomato paste and stir. Add spices to taste (increase the paprika for a sweeter taste or the cayenne for a spicier chili).
- Cover and simmer on stove top for 45 minutes to 1 hour.

SERVES 6 TO 8

NOTE: *If you want to add even more veggies to your chili, stir in 8 ounces sliced mushrooms along with the tomatoes.*

BEEF BOURGUIGNON

½ cup butter, divided
1 tablespoon brandy
1 cup flour, divided
2 pounds beef filet, cut into chunks
2 garlic cloves, minced
1 pound mushrooms, halved
6 small chopped white onions
2 cups beef stock
¾ cup Burgundy wine
2 tablespoons fresh parsley, chopped
1 teaspoon salt
1 teaspoon thyme
¼ teaspoon pepper
1 to 2 tablespoons Worcestershire sauce
Egg noodles

- In a heavy bottom frying pan, melt ¼ cup butter. Add brandy.
- Roll beef in ¾ cup flour until coated.
- Sear beef in butter and brandy until cooked rare. Transfer beef to a large cooking pot.
- Melt remaining butter in the frying pan and sauté garlic, mushrooms, and onions until cooked (5 to 7 minutes). Add the vegetables to the beef in the large pot.
- Stir in stock, wine, parsley, salt, thyme, and pepper. Simmer 2 hours.
- Cool the meat and vegetables in the pot. Thicken by stirring in ¼ cup flour and Worcestershire to taste. Bring back to a boil for at least 5 minutes until thick before serving.
- Serve over cooked egg noodles.

SERVES 6 TO 8

NOTE: *A classic French dish, this recipe can simmer in a pot and impress guests at a dinner party so you aren't stuck tending to dinner. Instead of noodles, it can also be served over boiled potatoes or rice.*

VEGGIE TORTILLA SOUP

8 cups vegetable broth

1 tablespoon butter

1 medium onion, chopped

1 summer squash, peeled and chopped

½ bunch cilantro, chopped

30 tortilla chips

1 teaspoon sugar

½ teaspoon ground cumin

½ poblano, chipotle, or jalapeño pepper (based on preference), seeded and diced

2 cups corn (frozen, canned, or fresh)

Juice of ½ lime

- In a large stock pot bring broth to a simmer over medium-high heat.
- In a separate saucepan, melt butter and sauté onion and squash. Add cilantro and tortilla chips to pan and add enough hot broth to cover (1 to 2 cups). Cover and simmer for 20 minutes until soft.
- Add sugar, cumin, and pepper of choice to squash pot mixture. Stir to combine.
- Using an immersion blender, purée mixture until smooth. (You can also use a regular blender and purée in small batches.)
- Add puréed mixture to the rest of the broth. Stir in corn and lime juice.

SERVES 6 TO 8

NOTE: *Even meat lovers can enjoy this hearty and spicy vegetarian soup. You can top with sliced avocado, sour cream or Greek yogurt, and cheese.*

SLOW COOKER VEGAN CHILI 

2 medium yellow onions, chopped

2 green bell peppers, chopped

8 garlic cloves, chopped

2 tablespoons chili powder

2 tablespoons ground cumin

4 teaspoons unsweetened cocoa powder

½ teaspoon ground cinnamon

2 teaspoons salt

1 teaspoon ground black pepper

1 can (28 ounces) fire-roasted diced tomatoes

1 can (28 ounces) plain diced tomatoes

2 cans (15 ounces) black beans, rinsed

2 cans (15 ounces) kidney beans, rinsed

3 medium sweet potatoes, peeled and cut into ½-inch pieces

2 cups water

- In a slow cooker, combine onion, bell pepper, garlic, chili powder, cumin, cocoa, cinnamon, salt, and pepper.
- Add the tomatoes (and their liquid), beans, sweet potatoes, and water.
- Cover and cook until the sweet potatoes are tender and the chili has thickened, on low for 7 to 8 hours or on high for 4 to 5 hours.
- Serve warm with tortilla chips, scallions, or sour cream (not vegan) on the side.

SERVES 8 TO 10

NOTE: *This is a popular dish at Junior League council meetings. The sweet potatoes, cocoa, and cinnamon give it a unique flavor that feels hearty and meaty while being a vegan dish. It's great to bring to a group when you don't know about dietary restrictions.*

HEARTY MINESTRONE SOUP

1 teaspoon olive oil

1 pound ground mild Italian sausage or turkey sausage

1½ cups yellow onion, chopped

2 cups carrots, ½-inch diced

2½ cups peeled butternut squash, cubed

1½ tablespoons minced garlic

2 teaspoons fresh thyme leaves (or 1 teaspoon dry), chopped

1 can (26 ounces) diced tomatoes, drained

6 to 8 cups low sodium chicken stock, divided

1 teaspoon salt

1½ teaspoons freshly ground black pepper

1 can (15 ounces) cannellini beans, drained and rinsed

2 cups small pasta, like Ditalini, cooked al dente

8 to 10 ounces fresh baby spinach (optional)

½ cup good dry white wine

Parmesan cheese, freshly grated

- Over medium heat, heat olive oil in a large stockpot. Remove sausage from casing and brown.

- Add the onions, carrots, squash, garlic, and thyme. Continue cooking, stirring occasionally for 8 to 10 minutes until vegetables soften.

- Add tomatoes, 6 cups chicken stock, salt, and pepper.

- Bring to a boil, then lower to simmer uncovered for 30 minutes until the vegetables are tender. Add the beans and cooked pasta, and heat through.

- The soup should be hearty. Add more chicken stock to the desired consistency.

- Just before serving, stir in spinach until just wilted. Finally stir in white wine and add additional salt and pepper to taste.

- Sprinkle soup in serving bowls with Parmesan cheese.

SERVES 6 TO 8

NOTE: *This is a very hearty dish and great served with warm, crusty bread. Freezes well as a base without the spinach and pasta. To serve, thaw and stir in spinach and pasta.*

HOLIDAY ICED SHORTBREAD COOKIES

COOKIE

3 cups all-purpose flour

¾ cup sugar

¼ teaspoon sea salt

¼ teaspoon cardamom (optional)

1½ cups butter, chilled and cut into ½-inch cubes

½ teaspoon rum extract

½ teaspoon almond extract

3 to 4 tablespoons cold water

ROYAL ICING

1 pound powdered sugar

5 tablespoons meringue powder

½ cup water

Food coloring of choice (optional)

COOKIE

- Preheat the oven to 325°F.
- Line a baking sheet with parchment paper.
- Whisk together the flour, sugar, salt, and cardamom in a large bowl. Cut in the butter using a pastry cutter until the mixture resembles coarse crumbs.
- In a small bowl, mix rum extract, almond extract, and water.
- Slowly mix the liquid mixture into the dry ingredients a little at a time, until the mixture holds together in a ball when you squeeze it.
- Place the dough onto a floured surface and sprinkle dough with flour. Roll the dough until it is about ¼-inch thick. Using cookie cutters of choice, cut the dough into shapes and place 1-inch apart on parchment lined baking sheet. Cover with plastic wrap and refrigerate for at least 20 to 30 minutes
- Remove plastic wrap and bake the cookies in preheated oven until the edges are lightly browned, 16 to 18 minutes. Allow the cookies to cool on the baking sheet for 2 to 3 minutes before moving to wire racks to cool completely.

ROYAL ICING

- While cooling, mix the icing ingredients together in a mixing bowl until they are smooth, for about 5 to 7 minutes.
- Once the cookies are completely cooled, ice them using the icing in an icing bag. Let sit a few hours until the icing hardens. Store cookies in an airtight container.

MAKES 3 TO 4 DOZEN

NOTE: *Use this recipe for holiday cookies or anytime you want decorated cookies. You can use both large and small cookie cutters. These cookies are great fun to make and decorate with kids or friends and family. If you don't have a rolling pin, large glass bottles with the labels removed make a great alternative!*

BUCKEYES

½ pound butter, melted
16 ounces smooth peanut butter
5½ cups powdered sugar

12 ounces semisweet chocolate chips
2 ounces paraffin wax, grated or chopped

- In a medium bowl (or electric stand mixer), blend melted butter and peanut butter until smooth.
- Mix in powdered sugar ½ cup at a time until smooth.
- Shape mixture into 1-inch balls and place on rimmed cookie sheet or a large plastic container. (Separate layers with parchment or wax paper.)
- Refrigerate balls overnight.
- In a small saucepan, melt chocolate chips and wax together over indirect heat (use a double boiler or a heat-safe bowl over a pot of boiling water).
- Using a toothpick, dip peanut butter balls into chocolate, leaving a small section of the peanut butter visible.
- Cool buckeyes on wax paper. Refrigerate or freeze in an airtight container.

MAKES APPROXIMATELY 75 CANDIES

PECAN CRESCENT COOKIES

1 cup pecans, finely chopped
1 cup butter
1 cup powdered sugar, divided
2 teaspoons vanilla

1 tablespoon water
½ teaspoon salt
2 cups flour

- Preheat oven to 350°F.
- Grind pecans in food processor until nearly crumb consistency.
- In a medium bowl, cream together butter and 4 tablespoons powdered sugar with an electric mixer. Stir in vanilla, water, and salt, and continue mixing until well-combined.
- Mix in flour. Fold in nuts.
- Shape into crescents, like a smile shape roughly the size (length and width) of one of your fingers.
- Bake for 15 minutes. Allow to cool completely.
- Roll cookies in remaining powdered sugar.

MAKES 24 TO 36 COOKIES

CHESS PIE

½ package (15 ounces) refrigerated pie crusts
Pie weights or dried beans
2 cups sugar
2 tablespoons cornmeal
1 tablespoon all-purpose flour
¼ teaspoon salt

½ cup butter or margarine, melted
¼ cup milk
1 tablespoon white vinegar
½ teaspoon vanilla
4 large eggs, lightly beaten

- Preheat oven to 425°F.

- Roll pie crust into a 9-inch pie plate according to package directions. Fold edges under and crimp. Line pie crust with aluminum foil, and fill with pie weights or dried beans.

- Parbake for 4 to 5 minutes. Remove weights and foil and bake 2 more minutes or until golden. Allow crust to cool. Reduce oven heat to 350°F.

- In a medium mixing bowl, stir together sugar, cornmeal, flour, salt, melted butter, milk, vinegar, and vanilla. Beat in eggs and mix well.

- Pour filling into pie crust.

- Bake at 350°F for 50 to 55 minutes until set. After 10 minutes, consider wrapping edges of pie crust in aluminum foil to prevent excessive browning.

- Cool completely on a wire rack.

SERVES 8 TO 10

NOTE: *Mix up this pie by stirring in 1 cup toasted flaked coconut before pouring into pie crust. Bake as directed above.*

NOTES

NOTES

SPRING

As winter melts away, spring showers bring beautiful flowers and greenery to Northern Virginia. With spring comes an abundance of bright vegetables like asparagus and peas that are show-stoppers on their own, or in pastas and risottos.

Bright fruits make a return and pair well with chicken [pages 100-102], jazz up a salad [pages 90-94], or sweeten up a dessert [pages 103-112]. Weekends are spent at outdoor sporting events, local gardens, or one of many wonderful Virginia wineries.

Pack a picnic with fresh dips and salsas or enjoy an afternoon tea with sandwiches and cakes, all highlighting the bright and fresh new bounty of spring.

What's Fresh In
SPRING?

Apricots

Artichokes

Asparagus

Avocados

Bananas

Broccoli

Cabbage

Carrots

Celery

Collard Greens

Garlic

Lettuce

Onions

Peas

Pineapple

Radishes

Strawberries

SPRING RECIPES

WAKE UP HAM, EGG, AND CHEESE CASSEROLE 

Nonstick spray
8 frozen hash brown patties
1 pound thick-cut ham, cubed
4 cups Cheddar cheese, shredded

7 eggs
1 cup milk
½ teaspoon salt
½ teaspoon ground mustard

- Preheat oven to 350°F.
- Spray a 9 x 13-inch casserole dish with nonstick spray.
- Place hash browns in a single layer on the bottom of the pan.
- Sprinkle the ham and cheese evenly over the hash browns.
- In a medium bowl, beat eggs, milk, salt, and mustard together.
- Pour mixture over the ham and cheese.
- Bake covered for 1 hour.
- Uncover and bake 15 minutes longer until the edges are golden brown.

SERVES 9 TO 12

NOTE: *This can be made the night before and baked in the morning. Be sure to remove from fridge 20 to 30 minutes prior to baking and allow to rest.*

BEST OF BOTH WORLDS DEVILED EGGS 

1 dozen large eggs
Large bowl of ice water
4 to 6 ounces mayonnaise, divided

2 to 3 ounces yellow mustard
Cajun seasoning to taste (at least ½ teaspoon)
Crab boil seasoning, for garnish

- Place eggs in a medium saucepan and cover with water.
- Bring eggs in water to a boil. Boil uncovered for 3 minutes.
- Remove pan from heat and cover.
- Let eggs sit covered for 12 minutes.
- Remove eggs from water and transfer to a large bowl of ice water. (This stops the eggs from cooking.) When eggs have cooled, transfer to refrigerator until ready to use.

DEVILED EGGS

- Chill hard-boiled eggs in the refrigerator before preparing. Carefully peel eggs and slice in half length-wise.
- Gently remove the egg yolks with a spoon and transfer to a small bowl. Set the egg white halves on a deviled egg tray or platter.
- Break up the yolks with a fork. Combine 4 ounces of mayonnaise with the yolks. Stir until combined.
- Add 2 ounces of yellow mustard and stir until combined. Add additional mustard and mayonnaise, alternating between both, until your desired consistency is reached. (The egg yolk mixture should be firm, but able to be piped through a pastry bag.) Finally stir in Cajun seasoning.
- When yolk mixture is seasoned to your preference, spoon into a pastry bag. Squeeze yolk mixture into each egg white half.
- Sprinkle finished deviled eggs with crab boil seasoning.

MAKES 24 DEVILED EGGS

NOTE: *If you don't have a pastry bag, use a plastic zip top sandwich bag, cutting off the tip of one corner for piping. These eggs can be made up to one day ahead, but are best served day of.*

TOMATO AND SALAMI CROSTINI 

4 ounces salami, sliced

¼ cup extra-virgin olive oil

1 tablespoon fresh lemon juice

½ teaspoon lemon zest, freshly grated

Salt and pepper to taste

1 garlic clove, minced

1 tablespoon parsley, chopped

1 tablespoon basil, chopped

4 large ripe tomatoes, thickly sliced

- Place salami in a shallow container.
- In a small bowl, combine oil, lemon juice, lemon zest, salt and pepper, garlic, parsley, and basil.
- Pour mixture over salami and let stand for 1 hour, turning once.
- Arrange overlapping slices of tomato and salami on a serving plate. Pour the remaining dressing over the top.
- Serve with crusty bread or on a bed of lettuce.

SERVES 6 TO 8 AS AN APPETIZER

Northern Virginia is home to a plethora of wineries, and spring is a great time to pack a picnic and enjoy the outdoors for the day. This dish is great to pack up and bring for a winery picnic or spread. Put together a small cheese platter and an assortment of breads and crackers, and crack open a bottle.

SPINACH AND ARTICHOKE DIP 

2 boxes (10 ounces) frozen spinach or 24 ounces fresh spinach

8 ounces cream cheese, softened

¼ cup mayonnaise

¼ cup sour cream

2 cups Parmesan cheese, grated

3 cans (14 ounces) artichoke hearts, drained and quartered

½ teaspoon garlic powder

½ teaspoon salt

- Preheat oven to 375°F.
- Prepare spinach. If using frozen, thaw and drain. If using fresh, sauté with water in large pan until wilted. Drain excess water.
- In a large bowl, combine cream cheese, mayonnaise, sour cream, and 1 cup grated cheese. Stir in spinach and artichoke hearts. Mix in garlic powder and salt to taste. Mix well.
- Pour dip into a large oven-safe dish (9 x 13-inch casserole or medium Dutch oven). Cover the top with remaining cup of cheese.
- Bake covered for 20 to 30 minutes.
- Serve hot with pita chips, bread/baguette, or raw vegetables.

SERVES 10 TO 12 AS AN APPETIZER

NOTE: *Want to lighten it up? Substitute plain, nonfat Greek yogurt for the sour cream and mayonnaise. Using fresh spinach adds a different dimension to this appetizer staple.*

ALL THE AVOCADOS GUACAMOLE 

2 ripe avocados, peeled and pitted

1 small Roma tomato, diced

¼ cup red onion, diced

1 garlic clove, minced

½ cup cilantro, chopped

Juice of 1 lime

½ teaspoon cumin

½ teaspoon salt

- In a medium bowl, mash avocado with a fork until mushy.
- Stir in tomato, onion, garlic, and cilantro until just combined.
- Add lime juice and seasonings. Adjust to taste.
- Serve with tortilla chips or fresh vegetables.

SERVES 4 TO 6 AS AN APPETIZER

NOTE: *This is an easy and simple guacamole, but the cumin and fresh lime take it up a notch. Enjoy at a backyard barbeque or with a taco dinner.*

EASY SPRING PEACH AND TOMATO SALSA 

2 medium tomatoes, diced

1 peach, peeled and diced

1 nectarine, peeled and diced

¼ cup Vidalia onion, diced

2 tablespoons fresh lime juice

3 tablespoons cilantro, chopped

¼ teaspoon cumin

Salt to taste

- Combine tomatoes, peach, nectarine, and onion in a large bowl.
- Toss with lime juice and cilantro. Season with cumin and salt to taste.
- Let the mixture sit for at least 15 minutes before serving, so flavors can marry.
- Salsa can be stored in the refrigerator in an airtight container for up to 2 days.
- Serve with corn chips, or on tacos or grilled fish.

SERVES 4 TO 6 AS AN APPETIZER

NOTE: *This is a big hit in the Junior League of Northern Virginia's Market Explorers program. It is easy for kids to help assemble this salsa and is enjoyed by grownups and children alike. If you like spicy sweet salsa, add a half jalapeño (seeded and chopped) for a little extra heat.*

MANDARIN ORANGE SALAD

1 tablespoon butter

¼ cup white sugar

¾ cup of slivered almonds

2 large heads of romaine lettuce, washed, dried, and chopped

3 to 4 scallions, chopped

2 to 3 celery stalks, chopped

2 cans (10 ounces) Mandarin oranges, drained, or 4 Mandarin oranges, peeled and sectioned

1 bottle (16 ounces) poppy seed dressing

- In a medium skillet, melt butter over medium heat. Stir in sugar until caramel consistency and add almonds. Stir with a wooden spoon until the sugar turns brown and the almonds start to smell toasted.

- Immediately turn the hot almonds onto wax paper to cool. Let almonds cool completely.

- When ready to serve, assemble lettuce, scallions, celery, drained or fresh Mandarin oranges, and caramelized almonds in a large salad bowl.

- Dress salad with desired amount of poppy seed salad dressing.

SERVES 10 TO 12

NOTE: *This is a great salad to bring to events. Wait to dress it until you arrive. It is also a great entrée salad. Just add grilled chicken or salmon.*

NANA'S TORTELLINI SALAD

DRESSING

¾ cup olive oil

3 tablespoons lemon juice, freshly squeezed

1 garlic clove, minced

SALAD

1 bag (16 ounces) tortellini (spinach and ricotta works well in this salad, but any flavor will work)

½ cup basil leaves, julienned

1 pint cherry or grape tomatoes, halved or quartered

4 ounces feta cheese, crumbled

Salt and pepper to taste

DRESSING

- Mix olive oil, lemon juice, and garlic together. Let sit for at least an hour, up to one day, before serving. Use a mason jar for easy mixing and pouring.

SALAD

- Cook tortellini according to package instructions. Drain thoroughly.
- In a large mixing or serving bowl, combine cooked tortellini, basil, and prepared dressing. Allow pasta mixture to cool to room temperature.
- Just before serving, mix in tomatoes and feta. Season with salt and pepper to taste.
- This salad is best served at room temperature.

SERVES 6

This pasta salad is simple enough that even kids love it. It's easy to make ahead of time for a party and is a great way to highlight beautiful tomatoes and fresh basil.

SPRING GRILLED CHICKEN SALAD WITH BALSAMIC VINAIGRETTE

CHICKEN

- ½ cup extra-virgin olive oil
- ½ cup cilantro leaves, chopped
- 3 tablespoons lemon juice
- 2 large garlic cloves, minced
- 1 teaspoon cumin
- 1 teaspoon sumac
- ½ teaspoon ground coriander
- ½ teaspoon cayenne pepper
- 1½ pounds boneless, skinless chicken breasts or chicken thighs

SALAD WITH BALSAMIC VINAIGRETTE

- 2 large pita breads, split horizontally
- 1½ cups balsamic vinegar
- 1 cup olive oil
- 2 tablespoons garlic, pressed
- 2 tablespoons parsley
- 1 tablespoon sugar, or to taste
- 1 tablespoon basil
- 2 teaspoons oregano
- Sea salt to taste
- Fresh ground black pepper to taste
- 1 large head romaine lettuce, cut into 1-inch strips
- 2 tablespoons mint, chopped
- ½ cup watercress
- ½ cup cilantro
- 1 cucumber, peeled and sliced
- 1 pound ripe tomatoes, diced
- 1½ teaspoons sumac

CHICKEN

- In a blender, combine olive oil, cilantro, lemon juice, garlic, cumin, sumac, coriander, and cayenne pepper. Purée until smooth.

- Pour marinade into a large plastic zip top bag. Add chicken and turn to coat.

- Refrigerate for at least 4 hours, preferably overnight. Heat grill to medium-high heat. Remove chicken reserving marinade for basting. Grill chicken, turning occasionally and basting with marinade until brown and cooked through.

- Transfer to a plate and loosely cover with aluminum foil. Let cool, then tear or cut into pieces.

SALAD

- Preheat oven to 300°F.

- Bake pita directly on rack for 10 minutes until dry and crisp, but not browned. Let cool and then break into 1-inch pieces.

- In a small bowl, combine balsamic vinegar, olive oil, garlic, parsley, sugar, basil, and oregano. Whisk until emulsified. Season with salt and pepper.

- In a large salad or serving bowl, mix lettuce, mint, watercress, cilantro, cucumber, tomatoes, and sumac.

- Toss with ½ cup of dressing. Stir in chicken and pita, adding more dressing as needed. Season with additional salt and pepper if needed.

SERVES 6 TO 8

NOTE: *This salad is a fresh herb and ingredient stunner. Not too heavy, it's bulked up with vegetables and a ton of chicken. Make it gluten-free by leaving out the pita.*

HAPPY TUNA SALAD 

1 can (6 ounces) tuna packed in water, thoroughly drained

1 tablespoon red onion, diced

2 tablespoons red pepper, diced

2 tablespoons yellow pepper, diced

2 tablespoons orange pepper, diced

¼ cup walnuts, roughly chopped

½ medium ripe avocado, mashed

1 lemon

Salt and pepper to taste

- In a medium bowl, combine tuna, onion, peppers, and walnuts.
- Mix until evenly distributed.
- Stir in mashed avocado. Finish with fresh lemon juice (this will limit the browning from the avocado). Add salt and pepper to taste.

SERVES 2

NOTE: *This is an easy, much healthier tuna salad that is great with crackers, or on a sandwich or salad. It's also great served on fresh tomato slices. Using avocado in place of mayonnaise saves a lot of calories and adds an extra dimension of flavor.*

GARLIC MASHED "POTATOES" 

1 medium head cauliflower

1 tablespoon cream cheese, softened

¼ cup Parmesan cheese, grated

1 to 2 teaspoons garlic, minced

1 teaspoon chicken broth paste or bouillon starter

Salt and pepper to taste

Chives, finely chopped

- Fill a medium saucepan with water and bring to a boil. Cut cauliflower into small pieces. Boil for 5 to 6 minutes, until tender.

- Drain well in a colander. Pat the cauliflower very dry, and do not let cool.

- Using a food processor or blender, purée the hot cauliflower with the cream cheese, Parmesan cheese, garlic, chicken broth, salt and pepper until almost smooth (you want some texture).

- Serve garnished with chives.

SERVES 4

NOTE: *A great alternative to starchy mashed potatoes, these garlic mashed potatoes are a great side for any meat or fish dish.*

OVEN-ROASTED ASPARAGUS

**1 bunch asparagus spears,
  thinly trimmed**
2 tablespoons olive oil
1 garlic clove, minced

1 teaspoon sea salt
½ teaspoon ground pepper
1 tablespoon lemon juice

- Preheat oven to 425°F.

- Place the asparagus in a mixing bowl and drizzle with olive oil. Toss to coat the spears, then sprinkle with garlic, salt, and pepper, and toss again.

- Arrange the asparagus in a single layer on a rimmed baking sheet.

- Bake in the preheated oven until just tender, 12 to 15 minutes depending on the thickness. Sprinkle with lemon juice just before serving.

SERVES 4 TO 6

NOTE: *"I didn't think I liked asparagus until I tried it this way."* You can also add 1 tablespoon of Parmesan cheese when you toss the asparagus with the olive oil for a twist. This is great with any meat or fish dish.

COLD DAN DAN NOODLES 

SAUCE

2 garlic cloves

3 tablespoons sesame oil

½ cup smooth peanut butter

¼ cup rice vinegar

¼ cup low sodium soy sauce

¼ cup sherry or Mirin rice wine

1½ teaspoons ginger paste or fresh ginger, peeled and roughly chopped

¼ to ½ teaspoon red pepper flakes or to taste

1 tablespoon brown sugar, packed

½ teaspoon kosher salt

¼ cup warm water

VEGETABLES AND NOODLES

12 ounces spaghetti, cooked

3 or 4 Persian cucumbers, julienned

1 cup carrots, shredded

6 green onions (green parts only), cut into long strips

1 red pepper (optional), julienned

1 tablespoon sesame seeds, roasted (optional)

3 tablespoons cilantro leaves (optional)

- Combine all sauce ingredients in a blender or food processor. Blend until well-combined (about 90 seconds).

- Mix the sauce, noodles, and vegetables together in a large serving bowl and adjust for seasoning.

- Garnish with cilantro and sesame seeds, if using.

- Serve at room temperature or cold.

SERVES 6

NOTE: *You can add protein to this dish, such as tempeh or tofu for vegans, or chicken or shrimp for non-vegetarians. This recipe can be made gluten-free by using gluten-free spaghetti or shirataki noodles, and substituting tamari for the soy sauce. If you are making this for children and have concerns about the rice wine, it can be omitted and will still be very tasty.*

SIMPLE WEEKNIGHT SALMON

4 salmon filets with skin on (3 to 4 ounces each)

6 tablespoons olive oil

3 tablespoons low-sodium soy sauce

2 tablespoons Dijon mustard

1 tablespoon garlic, minced

- Preheat oven to 350°F.
- Lightly spray a 9 x 13-inch baking dish with nonstick spray.
- Place salmon filets skin-side down.
- In a small bowl, whisk together olive oil, soy sauce, mustard, and garlic.
- Pour evenly over each filet, reserving a few tablespoons for dipping.
- Bake uncovered for 10 to 12 minutes, or until salmon is easily flaked.
- Serve with remaining sauce on the side.

SERVES 4

PORK TENDERLOIN AND BLUEBERRY SAUCE

1 pound pork tenderloin

2 tablespoons butter

1 large sweet onion, thinly sliced

½ teaspoon salt

¼ teaspoon ground black pepper

2 tablespoons sugar

¼ cup port wine (can substitute sweet sherry)

2 tablespoons balsamic vinegar

1 cup fresh blueberries

- Preheat broiler.
- Broil pork, turning occasionally until cooked through, for about 20 minutes.
- Move pork to platter and cover to keep warm.
- While broiling pork, in a large skillet, melt butter over medium-high heat.
- Add onions, salt, and pepper to skillet. Sauté until onions are golden brown, about 10 minutes.
- Add sugar to onions and continue cooking until onions are caramelized, about 5 minutes longer.
- Stir in port, vinegar, and blueberries to onions and bring to a boil. Remove from heat and allow sauce to thicken.
- Thinly slice pork and serve with sauce.

SERVES 4

NOTE: *This recipe was developed after stopping at a "you pick" blueberry farm on the way home from the beach. It has become a spring favorite!*

SIRLOIN STEAKS WITH ROASTED POTATOES AND GREEN BEANS

ROASTED POTATOES

1 pound Yukon gold potatoes, cut into bite-sized pieces

¼ cup olive oil

Salt and pepper to taste

¼ teaspoon thyme

STEAKS AND GREEN BEANS

4 sirloin steaks (about 6 ounces each)

Salt and pepper

1 tablespoon olive oil

4 tablespoons butter, divided

3 garlic cloves, halved

1 shallot, thinly sliced, roughly chopped

12 ounces fresh green beans

1 pint cherry tomatoes, halved

1 lemon, quartered and seeded

ROASTED POTATOES

- Preheat oven to 475°F.
- In a large bowl, toss potatoes with olive oil, salt, pepper, and thyme.
- Place potatoes on rimmed baking sheet.
- Roast 20 to 25 minutes until browned.

STEAKS AND GREEN BEANS

- Pat the steaks dry and season with salt and pepper on both sides.
- In a large pan, heat olive oil and 2 tablespoons butter over medium-high heat.
- Add steaks and garlic halves to the pan. Cook steaks to desired wellness. Occasionally stir garlic halves so they do not burn.
- Once the steaks are cooked, remove from pan and cover. Leave the garlic halves in the pan.
- Reduce heat to medium and add water, scraping off bits stuck to the pan. Melt 2 tablespoons butter.
- Sauté shallots, green beans, and tomatoes. Cover the pan and cook until the green beans are tender. Finally squeeze the half lemon and stir.
- Divide potatoes, veggies, and steaks, and serve.

SERVES 4

GRANDMA'S CHICKEN ADOBO 

1 tablespoon olive oil

¼ yellow onion, diced

1 garlic clove, minced

1 bay leaf

2 boneless, skinless chicken thighs, cubed

2 tablespoons distilled white or balsamic vinegar

2 tablespoons soy sauce

½ cup water

½ tablespoon brown sugar, packed

Salt and pepper to taste

Cooked rice, for serving

- Heat olive oil in a saucepan over medium heat.
- Sauté onion until translucent, about 5 to 7 minutes.
- Add garlic and bay leaf and sauté for 30 seconds.
- Add chicken and sauté until no longer pink, about 5 minutes.
- Add vinegar, soy sauce, water, and brown sugar, and cook until sauce thickens slightly, about 10 minutes.
- Add salt and pepper to taste.
- Serve over cooked rice.

SERVES 2

NOTE: *This recipe serves two, but can easily be doubled or more to serve a crowd. It is a Filipino dish, easy enough to make on a weeknight and always enjoyed by guests.*

UKULELE PHIL AND THE HULA KIDS' HULI HULI CHICKEN

1 pound boneless, skinless chicken thighs

HULI HULI SAUCE

¼ cup ketchup

¼ cup shoyu (Japanese soy sauce)

½ cup chicken broth

⅓ cup white wine

¼ cup frozen pineapple juice concentrate

Pinch of fresh or dried ginger

½ teaspoon Worcestershire sauce

- In a medium bowl, combine ketchup, shoyu, broth, wine, pineapple juice, ginger, and Worcestershire sauce.
- Add chicken thighs to bowl and let marinate for 30 minutes to 1 hour.
- Grill on medium-high, turning and basting with sauce until cooked completely (about 40 minutes).
- Continue basting so cooked chicken is covered in a nice glaze.

SERVES APPROXIMATELY 4

Ukulele Phil and the Hula Kids have performed for many years at the Junior League of Northern Virginia's holiday celebration, *The Enchanted Forest*. This flavorful spring dish is a go-to year-round.

CHICKEN BREASTS STUFFED WITH PROSCIUTTO AND PARMIGIANO-REGGIANO

4 chicken breast halves (6 ounce)

Salt and pepper to taste

4 slices prosciutto, halved (preferably imported)

Several thin slices Parmigiano-Reggiano cheese

¼ cup fresh parsley, chopped

2 tablespoons extra-virgin olive oil

2 tablespoons butter, divided

½ cup white wine or water

2 tablespoons balsamic vinegar

- Preheat the oven to 400°F.
- Place each chicken breast piece between two sheets of plastic wrap and pound firmly with a mallet or other object (a can works) until evenly flattened and less than ¼-inch thick.
- Season chicken with salt (not too much since both the prosciutto and Parmigiano-Reggiano are salty) and pepper.
- Layer a couple of pieces of prosciutto, some Parmigiano-Reggiano, and a good sprinkling of parsley on each piece of chicken.
- Roll up and, if necessary, skewer with a toothpick or two (or use kitchen twine to tie).
- Heat a large ovenproof skillet over medium-high heat.
- Heat olive oil and 1 tablespoon butter until butter foam subsides.
- Brown rolled up chicken in the pan on each side for 3 to 4 minutes.
- Move the pan to preheated oven.
- Cook until chicken rolls are done, about 15 minutes (they will be lightly browned and quite firm when done, but it's safest to cut into one to be sure the meat is no longer bright pink).
- Move chicken to a cutting board and let rest.
- Put the skillet back on top of stove over medium-high heat. Add wine (or water) and cook, stirring and scraping the bottom of the pan, until liquid is all but evaporated.
- Stir in vinegar and reduce by half, just a couple of minutes.
- Stir in remaining 1 tablespoon butter until it melts. Taste and adjust seasoning.
- Cut rolls into 1-inch slices, and arrange on a serving platter. Top with sauce and serve.

SERVES 4

KENTUCKY PIE 

½ (15 ounces) package refrigerated pie crusts

1½ cups pecans or walnuts, chopped

1 cup (6 ounces) semisweet chocolate chips

1 cup dark corn syrup

½ cup sugar

½ cup brown sugar, firmly packed

¼ cup bourbon or water

4 large eggs

¼ cup butter or margarine, melted

2 teaspoons cornmeal

2 teaspoons vanilla extract

½ teaspoon salt

- Preheat oven to 325°F.
- Fit pie crust into a 9-inch, deep-dish pie plate according to package directions; fold edges under, and crimp.
- Sprinkle pecans or walnuts and chocolate chips evenly onto bottom of pie crust. Set aside.
- In a large saucepan, combine corn syrup, sugar, brown sugar, and bourbon. Bring to a boil over medium heat.
- Cook, stirring constantly for 3 minutes, then remove from heat.
- In a separate bowl, whisk together eggs, butter, cornmeal, vanilla, and salt. Gradually whisk about one-fourth hot mixture into egg mixture. Pour egg mixture into remaining hot mixture, whisking constantly.
- Pour filling into prepared pie crust.
- Bake for 55 minutes or until set. Cool on wire rack.

SERVES 8

The original Derby Pie (also known as Kentucky Pie) was created in celebration of the horse race. This pie is a delightful treat for a spring party or any gathering.

NANNY MARTIN'S LEMON POUND CAKE 

1 cup (2 sticks) butter
½ cup vegetable shortening
3 cups sugar
5 eggs
½ teaspoon baking powder

3 cups all-purpose flour
1 cup milk
1 tablespoon vanilla extract
1 tablespoon lemon extract

- Preheat oven to 325°F.
- Grease two 9-inch bread pans.
- In a large mixing bowl, cream butter and shortening together using an electric mixer.
- Add sugar and mix well.
- Add eggs, one at a time, beating after each.
- In a separate bowl, sift together baking powder and flour.
- Add to butter mixture, gradually alternating dry mix and milk until incorporated.
- Stir in extracts.
- Pour into pans.
- Bake for 80 minutes until a toothpick comes out clean. Allow to cool.

MAKES 2 LOAVES

Nanny Martin made her famous pound cake every Sunday afternoon after church. "You never know who's going to stop by [during the week]," she would say. Now her recipe is a go-to cake for celebrations, holidays, and comfort food.

AFTERNOON TEA CAKES 

1 cup butter, softened
1¼ cups sugar
¾ cup golden syrup (can be purchased online if not available in stores)

1 tablespoon vanilla extract
2 teaspoons lemon juice
3 eggs
4½ cups self-rising flour

- Preheat oven to 350°F.
- Line baking sheets with parchment paper.
- In a large bowl, cream together butter and sugar with an electric mixer.
- Add golden syrup, vanilla extract, and lemon juice, beating until just blended.
- Add eggs, one at a time, beating until just blended after each.
- Gradually add flour, beating until blended after each addition.
- Drop dough by rounded spoonfuls 2-inches apart onto prepared baking sheets.
- Bake for 8 to 10 minutes or until edges are golden brown.
- Transfer to wire racks and allow to cool completely.
- Store in an airtight container for up to a week, or freeze for up to 4 weeks.

MAKES 8 TO 12 TEA CAKES

NOTE: *As the name suggests, this treat is best enjoyed with afternoon tea.*

BONNIE'S IRISH CRÈME BUNDT CAKE

CAKE

Nonstick spray

1 box (15 ounces) yellow or chocolate cake mix

1 box (3 ounces) instant vanilla pudding mix

4 eggs

½ cup vegetable oil

¾ cup Irish cream liqueur

GLAZE

1 cup sifted powdered sugar

3 to 4 tablespoons Irish cream liqueur

CAKE

- Preheat oven to 350°F.
- Spray a 10-inch Bundt or tube pan with nonstick cooking spray.
- In a large bowl, combine cake mix, pudding mix, eggs, and oil.
- Beat with an electric mixer on medium speed for 2 minutes.
- Add liqueur, and beat another 30 seconds.
- Pour into prepared pan.
- Bake in a preheated oven for 50 minutes.
- Cool in pan for 10 minutes prior to turning on to a plate.

GLAZE

- Mix glaze in a bowl and stir with a fork. Use fork to drape glaze over cake when completely cooled.
- Sift powdered sugar atop glaze once dried.

SERVES 12 TO 16

NOTE: *This is always a hit for parties and celebrations. Brighten it up by using a few drops of food coloring in the glaze. Vanilla or chocolate cake, this decadent treat can also be cut up and frozen for up to 3 months.*

STRAWBERRY CAKE BALLS

1 box (15 ounces) strawberry cake mix

1 container (12 ounces) strawberry frosting

2 bags (11 ounces) white chocolate chips

Sprinkles (optional)

- Bake cake mix according to package directions and let cool completely.
- In a large bowl, break up into small pieces and mix with frosting.
- Refrigerate overnight.
- The next day, roll into balls and freeze overnight.
- Finally, melt chocolate chips (can melt in microwave or over double boiler).
- Using a fork, dip balls one at a time into chocolate.
- Place on wax paper to cool.
- If desired, top balls with sprinkles for extra decoration.

MAKES ABOUT 2 DOZEN CAKE BALLS

NOTE: *Try any cake and frosting pair. Kids will enjoy the decorating!*

COLA CAKE

CAKE

Nonstick spray
1 cup (2 sticks) butter
3 heaping tablespoons cocoa powder
1 cup cola (diet or regular)
2 cups flour

2 cups sugar
½ cup buttermilk
2 eggs, beaten
1 teaspoon baking soda
1 teaspoon vanilla extract
½ cup mini-marshmallows

ICING

½ cup (1 stick) butter or margarine
3 tablespoons cocoa powder

6 tablespoons cola
1 box (1 pound) powdered sugar

CAKE

- Preheat oven to 350°F.
- Spray a 10 x 15-inch cake pan with nonstick spray.
- In a saucepan, combine butter, cocoa powder, and cola.
- Heat to boiling until just combined.
- Transfer to a large bowl.
- Add flour and sugar to cola mixture. Mix well.
- Stir in buttermilk, beaten eggs, and baking soda. Mix well.
- Add vanilla extract and mini-marshmallows, stirring until just combined. The batter will be thin.
- Spread batter in pan and bake for 35 to 40 minutes. (A smaller pan can be used, but will take longer.)

ICING

- In a saucepan, combine butter, cocoa powder, cola, and powdered sugar.
- Heat over medium heat until smooth (3 to 5 minutes).
- Pour over cake right when it is out of the oven.

SERVES 12 TO 15

NOTE: *An old classic, this cola cake is always a crowd pleaser. Dress it up with sprinkles or chopped nuts, then bring it to a party and wait for the "Oohs" and "Ahhs."*

RECIPE ON NEXT PAGE

LEMON BLUEBERRY BUNDT CAKE

Nonstick spray

2½ cups plus 1 tablespoon all-purpose flour

2 teaspoons baking powder

½ teaspoon salt

1 cup (2 sticks) unsalted butter, softened

1 cup brown sugar

1 cup sugar

4 large eggs

1 tablespoon vanilla extract

1 tablespoon lemon juice

1 cup nonfat Greek yogurt

1 pint blueberries

1 tablespoon lemon zest

Powdered sugar for topping

- Preheat oven to 350°F.
- Prepare a 10-cup Bundt pan by spraying with nonstick spray.
- In a large bowl, sift together 2½ cups flour, baking powder, and salt.
- In a large mixing bowl or the bowl of a stand mixer, cream together butter and both sugars.
- Beat in eggs until mixture is well-combined and fluffy.
- Fold in vanilla and lemon juice.
- Alternate adding flour mixture and Greek yogurt to butter and sugar mixture. Beat on low until well-combined. Batter will be thick.
- In a small bowl, toss blueberries with additional 1 tablespoon flour and lemon zest.
- Gently fold blueberries into cake batter, being careful not to break.
- Pour batter into prepared cake pan.
- Bake 65 to 75 minutes. Test with a toothpick. Cake is done when it comes out clean.
- Allow to sit in pan for 30 minutes to 1 hour.
- Turn over on to wire rack to cool completely.
- Dust with powdered sugar before serving.

SERVES 12 TO 14

This cake is perfect for spring, highlighting fresh lemon and blueberries. Don't have blueberries? Try strawberries or blackberries instead. The Greek yogurt gives this cake a great density.

BEST (ANYTHING) COOKIES 

¾ cup vegetable shortening

1½ cups dark brown sugar

1 tablespoon milk

2 tablespoons vanilla extract

1 egg

2 cups all-purpose flour

1 teaspoon salt

1 teaspoon baking soda

12 ounces (about 2 cups) semisweet chocolate chips or a favorite filling

- Preheat oven to 350°F.
- In a large bowl, combine shortening, sugar, milk, vanilla extract, and egg. Beat together on medium speed.
- Stir in flour, salt, and baking soda until well-combined.
- Fold in chocolate chips or your favorite filling.
- Use a tablespoon cookie scoop to drop on to an ungreased cookie sheet about 2-inches apart.
- Bake for 10 minutes.
- Cool cookies completely on a wire rack.

MAKES 24 COOKIES

NOTE: *These cookies are great for any season. Even if you've never made chocolate chip cookies from scratch, these are simple and always a hit. They are anything cookies because you can use any kind of filling: chocolate chips, oatmeal and raisin, chopped up candy, dried fruit, or any of your favorite cookie pieces.*

BLACK RUSSIAN CAKE

1 package (18.25 ounces) yellow cake mix

1 package (5.1 ounces) instant chocolate pudding mix

4 large eggs

1 cup vegetable oil

½ cup vodka

½ cup water

½ cup sugar

½ cup coffee liqueur, divided

½ cup powdered sugar

- Preheat oven to 350°F.
- Beat first 7 ingredients and ¼ cup coffee liqueur at medium speed with an electric mixer until smooth; pour into a greased and floured Bundt pan.
- Bake at 350°F for 50 minutes.
- Combine remaining ¼ cup coffee liqueur and powdered sugar, stirring until smooth.
- Let cake cool slightly.
- Remove cake from pan.
- Puncture cake surface with a large wooden pick and brush with glaze.
- Let harden.

SERVES 16

This cake is the most discussed recipe from our last cookbook! It's legendary and there is always a reason to make it.

NOTES

NOTES

SUMMER

Northern Virginia summers may be hot, but they are a time of fun and excitement. Whether driving to a nearby beach, hiking local trails, or enjoying a backyard barbecue or neighborhood pool party, there is something for everyone.

Summer fruits and vegetables can find a way into your kitchen as breakfast, lunch, dinner, dessert, or even a drink. Start busy (or lazy) summer days with berry breakfasts [page 124] or egg casseroles [page 126].

Fuel up with superfood-studded salads and delicious sides like pasta salad and potato salad to bring to any house party. Round out your evening with fantastic grilling that everyone is sure to enjoy.

Whip up a few slushy drinks to cool you down from the heat [page 148] or indulge in red, white, and blue desserts (pages 146-147) that celebrate both the season and our nation.

What's Fresh In
SUMMER?

Blackberries

Blueberries

Carrots

Celery

Cherries

Corn

Cucumbers

Eggplant

Garlic

Green Beans

Kiwis

Mangoes

Melons (Cantaloupe, Honeydew, Watermelon)

Nectarines

Okra

Peaches

Plums

Raspberries

Strawberries

Summer Squash and Zucchini

Tomatillos

Tomatoes

SUMMER RECIPES

CREAM CHEESE COFFEE CAKE 

CAKE

1 cup butter	2 cups flour
1 cup sugar	2 teaspoons baking powder
2 eggs	½ teaspoon salt

CAKE FILLING

16 ounces cream cheese	1 cup sugar
1 egg yolk	1 teaspoon vanilla

CAKE TOPPING SPRINKLE

¼ cup sugar	¼ cup butter, melted
¾ cup flour	

CAKE

- Preheat oven to 350°F.
- Grease a 9 x 13-inch cake pan.
- In a large mixing bowl, cream together butter and sugar with an electric beater.
- Add one egg at a time and beat well.
- Slowly add flour, baking powder, and salt to mixture. Mix batter well.
- Spread about ⅔ of batter into the bottom of the prepared cake pan.

CAKE FILLING

- In a medium bowl, mix cream cheese, egg yolk, sugar, and vanilla.
- Beat until well combined.
- Spread over cake.
- Drop the remaining ⅓ of cake batter in large spoonfuls over top of the filling.

CAKE TOPPING SPRINKLE

- In a small bowl, mix together sugar, flour, and melted butter with a spoon, fork, or your hands until crumbly.
- Top cake with the crumbles.
- Bake in preheated oven for 45 minutes.

SERVES 9 TO 12

NOTE: *This is best served warm, but it is still delicious served cold. This coffee cake is also yummy with fresh berries or preserves. Spread them on top of the cake filling before adding the remaining cake batter.*

HUNT BREAKFAST COFFEE CAKE

CAKE

½ cup plus 2 teaspoons of butter

1½ cups packed light brown sugar

2 large eggs

2 cups all-purpose flour (can substitute whole wheat flour if you prefer)

1 teaspoon cinnamon

½ teaspoon salt

1 teaspoon baking soda

1 cup sour cream

1 teaspoon vanilla extract

2 cups peeled, cored, and chopped apples

½ cup chopped walnuts

TOPPING

½ cup brown sugar

½ cup all-purpose flour

½ teaspoon cinnamon

4 tablespoons butter, softened

GLAZE

½ cup packed brown sugar

2 tablespoons water

½ teaspoon vanilla

CAKE

- Preheat oven to 350°F .
- Lightly grease a 9 x 13-inch glass baking dish with 2 tablespoons of butter.
- In a large bowl, cream together butter and sugar until light and fluffy.
- Add eggs one at a time, beating after each addition.
- In another bowl, sift together flour, cinnamon, salt, and baking soda.
- Add to wet ingredients, alternating with sour cream and vanilla.
- Fold in apples and walnuts.
- Pour into baking dish, spreading batter to the edges.

TOPPING

- In a medium bowl, combine sugar, flour, cinnamon, and butter. Mix until it resembles large crumbs. Sprinkle topping over cake and bake 35 to 40 minutes until golden brown.
- Remove from oven and cool on wire rack for at least 10 minutes.

GLAZE

- In a small bowl, combine sugar, water, and vanilla extract. Whisk until smooth. Drizzle on cake and let harden slightly. Serve warm if possible.

SERVES 12

NOTE: *This coffee cake gets rave reviews at fox hunt breakfasts in Virginia. A decadent treat, it's also great for weekend guests or a Saturday brunch.*

BASIC BREAKFAST CASSEROLE

12 large eggs

1 loaf crusty bread (French or Italian work well), torn or cut into 1 to 2-inch pieces

2 cups shredded Cheddar cheese

1 cup milk

1 pound breakfast sausage

1 teaspoon paprika

Salt and pepper to taste

- In a large zip top bag, combine 12 eggs, torn bread, cheese, and milk.
- Shake the bag until mixed well.
- Store bag in refrigerator for 4 hours or overnight.
- When ready to bake, preheat oven to 375°F.
- Spray a 9 x 13-inch casserole dish with nonstick spray.
- Brown sausage in a large skillet according to instructions. Drain fat.
- Dump contents of zip top back into a large mixing bowl. Gently fold in cooked sausage and paprika. Add salt and pepper to taste.
- Spread mixture into prepared casserole dish.
- Bake uncovered for 45 minutes until set.

SERVES 8 TO 12

NOTE: *This can be made the night before and baked in the morning. Be sure to remove from fridge 20 to 30 minutes prior to baking and allow to rest. Lighten this up by using skim milk, reduced-fat cheese, and 6 whole eggs and 1½ cups liquid egg substitute. Try spicy sausage, turkey sausage, or even chicken sausage.*

BERRY BREAKFAST CASSEROLE 

6 eggs

1½ cups milk

2 teaspoons cinnamon

1 tablespoon vanilla extract

**1 loaf crusty French bread,
cut into 2-inch cubes**

**8 ounces cream cheese,
cut into cubes**

**2 cups berries
(blueberries, raspberries, or
blackberries all work well)**

⅓ cup sugar

- Spray a 9 x 13-inch casserole dish with nonstick cooking spray.
- In a large bowl, whisk together eggs, milk, cinnamon, and vanilla.
- Spread half of cut bread in the casserole dish.
- Top bread with cut up cream cheese and 1 cup of berries.
- Top with remaining half of cut bread and remaining 1 cup of berries.
- Pour egg mixture evenly on top of bread.
- Cover casserole dish and refrigerate for 4 hours or overnight.
- When ready to bake, preheat oven to 375°F.
- Uncover casserole and sprinkle sugar evenly across top.
- Cover tightly with foil and bake for 30 minutes.
- Remove foil and bake for another 30 minutes.
- Serve warm.

SERVES 8 TO 12

NOTE: *This also makes a great dessert served with a scoop of vanilla ice cream.*

GRAM'S CRÊPES

1 cup flour

½ teaspoon salt

3 large eggs

1½ cups milk (1 or 2 percent)

1 teaspoon vanilla

1 tablespoon sugar
(for dessert crêpes)

Butter or nonstick cooking
spray

Filling of your choice

- In a medium bowl, whisk flour and salt together. If making a sweet crêpe, add sugar as well. Set aside.
- In a large bowl, mix eggs, milk, and vanilla together.
- Slowly add flour and salt mixture to egg mixture and mix until fully combined.
- Heat a medium-large nonstick frying pan to medium.
- Use enough butter (or nonstick spray) to lightly coat the pan.
- When butter is melted and the pan is hot, ladle ¼ to ⅓ cup of batter into the middle of the pan.
- Swirl pan to spread batter evenly.
- After about 2 minutes, the underside of the crêpe should be lightly browned and ready to flip. Flip using a large spatula.
- Cook the other side for about a minute and move to a plate. (Crêpes can be tricky to make, but after a few they get easier.)
- Fill crêpes with filling of choice and serve.

MAKES 4 TO 6 CRÊPES

NOTE: *Crêpes can be sweet or savory. For a sweet treat, try fresh berries and whipped cream or bananas and chocolate sauce. For something savory, try eggs and cheese or chicken and pesto.*

BACON AND EGG CASSEROLE

4 strips bacon

18 eggs

1 cup milk

1 cup shredded Cheddar cheese

1 cup sour cream

¼ cup green onions, sliced

1 teaspoon salt

½ teaspoon pepper

- Preheat oven to 325°F.
- Spray a 9 x 13-inch baking dish with nonstick spray.
- In a large skillet, cook bacon over medium heat until crisp.
- Move bacon to paper towel and drain grease.
- In a large bowl, beat eggs.
- Add milk, cheese, sour cream, green onions, salt, and pepper. Mix well.
- Pour egg mixture into prepared baking dish.
- Crumble bacon and sprinkle on top.
- Bake uncovered in preheated oven for 40 to 45 minutes or until knife inserted near the center comes out clean.
- Let stand for 5 minutes before serving.

SERVES 9 TO 12

JALAPEÑO RANCH DIP 

2 cups plain, non-fat Greek yogurt

1 packet (1 ounce) dry ranch dressing dip mix

½ cup jarred jalapeños (if using fresh, use 1 large jalapeño with most seeds removed)

¼ cup cilantro

Juice of 1 lime

- Combine Greek yogurt, ranch dressing mix, jalapeños, cilantro, and lime juice in a food processor or blender.
- Blend until smooth and ingredients are combined.
- Refrigerate until serving.

MAKES 2 CUPS OF DIP

NOTE: *Serve with chips or veggies as an appetizer or serve as a sauce with tacos or grilled chicken. Can store in the fridge for up to one week, but it gets spicier the longer it sits.*

TEXAS CAVIAR 

2 cans (15 ounces) black beans, drained and rinsed

1 cup corn (fresh or frozen)

4 roma tomatoes, seeded and chopped

1 orange bell pepper, seeded and chopped

4 scallions, sliced

1 teaspoon garlic, minced

2 tablespoons fresh parsley, chopped

½ cup Italian dressing

Corn chips for serving

- Mix black beans, corn, tomatoes, bell pepper, scallions, garlic, 1 tablespoon parsley, and Italian dressing together in container with tight seal.

- Marinate in refrigerator at least 2 hours, shaking or stirring once.

- Serve with corn chips and 1 tablespoon parsley garnish.

MAKES ABOUT 3 CUPS OF DIP; SERVES 6 TO 8 AS AN APPETIZER

NOTE: *This is a great, easy-to-make appetizer that works for people with all varieties of dietary restrictions. This is a great, easy-to-make appetizer or side dish that works for people with all varieties of dietary restrictions.*

TROPICAL SALAD WITH PINEAPPLE VINAIGRETTE 

6 slices bacon

¼ cup and 2 tablespoons pineapple juice

3 tablespoons rice wine vinegar

¼ cup light extra virgin olive oil

¼ teaspoon fresh ginger, grated

¼ teaspoon fresh garlic, minced

½ teaspoon sugar

Salt and pepper to taste

1 large head romaine lettuce, chopped

1 cup fresh pineapple, diced

½ cup macadamia nuts, chopped

3 green onions, thinly sliced

¼ cup shredded coconut, toasted

- Over medium heat, cook bacon in a large skillet until crisp. Remove to paper towel and drain. Crumble bacon and set aside.
- In a jar with lid or food processor, combine pineapple juice, vinegar, oil, ginger, garlic, sugar, salt, and pepper. Cover and shake well or blend until well combined.
- In a large salad bowl, toss together lettuce, pineapple, nuts, onions, and bacon.
- Pour enough dressing over salad to coat and toss.
- Garnish with toasted coconut.

SERVES 4 TO 6

NOTE: *Dressing keeps well in the fridge for a week. Use leftovers to marinate salmon or chicken before grilling.*

SUPERFOOD SALAD WITH LEMON VINAIGRETTE 

SALAD

½ cup dry quinoa

1 pound small to medium shrimp

⅓ cup red onion, chopped

1 orange, peeled and chopped

1 avocado, chopped

1 cup canned black beans, rinsed and drained

1 cup pomegranate seeds (from about 1 pomegranate)

1 cup corn, fresh or canned

⅓ cup cilantro, chopped

Salt and pepper

LEMON VINAIGRETTE

Juice of 2 lemons (or ¼ cup)

2 garlic cloves, microplaned or finely minced

Dash of sweetener (agave nectar, stevia, or sugar)

Salt and pepper

6 tablespoons extra virgin olive oil

SALAD

- Cook quinoa according to package directions. Set aside to cool.

- Bring a large pot of water to boil. When water is boiling, remove pot from heat and add shrimp. Cover and let sit for 5 minutes until shrimp are pink and cooked.

- Move cooked shrimp to an ice bath to stop cooking. Drain and dry on a paper towel.

LEMON VINAIGRETTE

- In a jar with a lid, combine lemon juice, garlic, sweetener, salt and pepper, and olive oil.

- Shake to combine.

- In a large bowl, combine cooled quinoa with red onion, orange segments, avocado, beans, pomegranate seeds, corn, cilantro, salt, and pepper.

- Stir in shrimp.

- Pour vinaigrette over the salad and stir to combine.

- Serve cold or at room temperature.

SERVES 6 TO 8 AS A SIDE DISH OR 4 AS AN ENTRÉE

This is a fantastic summer salad and a hit at any party or dinner. It keeps well in the fridge for 2 to 3 days.

CORN AND EDAMAME SALAD

2 cups shelled edamame, fresh or frozen

2 cups corn, fresh or frozen

1 green onion, sliced

1 red bell pepper, seeded and chopped

3 tablespoons cilantro, finely chopped

2 tablespoons garlic, minced

1½ tablespoons olive oil

1 tablespoon fresh lemon juice

1 tablespoon fresh lime juice

¼ teaspoon salt

⅛ teaspoon fresh ground black pepper

- In a large bowl, combine edamame, corn, green onion, red pepper, and cilantro.
- In a small bowl, whisk together garlic, olive oil, lemon juice, lime juice, salt, and black pepper until emulsified.
- Drizzle mixture over salad mixture and toss to coat.
- Cover and chill for at least 2 hours.

SERVES 6 TO 8 AS A SIDE

NOTE: *Even kids love this veggie-studded salad with the buttery fresh taste of edamame. If using frozen veggies, mix the salad frozen and let it sit in the fridge a bit longer to thaw.*

BLACK BEAN SALSA 

2 cans (15 ounces) black beans, drained

1 can (17 ounces) reduced-sodium, whole kernel corn, drained

2 large tomatoes, seeded and chopped

½ to 1 purple onion, chopped

¼ cup fresh cilantro, chopped

¼ cup lime juice

2 tablespoons olive oil

2 tablespoons red wine vinegar

¼ teaspoon ground red pepper

Salt and pepper to taste

1 large avocado, peeled and chopped

- Combine first 10 ingredients, stirring well.
- Chill until ready to serve.
- Stir in avocado when ready to serve.
- Garnish with avocado slices or fresh parsley sprigs, if desired.
- Serve with tortilla chips or as a side dish.

SERVES 10-12 AS AN APPETIZER, 6 AS A SIDE DISH

NOTE: *This is another fan favorite from our first cookbook. Add this salsa to traditional or breakfast tacos to take them up a notch.*

GREEK QUINOA SALAD

½ cup quinoa

1 cup vegetable broth

1 cup cherry tomatoes, quartered

½ cup feta cheese, crumbled

1 cup cucumber, seeded and diced

¼ cup red onion, diced

¼ cup Kalamata olives, pitted and chopped

1 teaspoon lemon pepper

1 tablespoon fresh dill, chopped

Juice of 1 lemon

- Cook quinoa according to package instructions using vegetable broth instead of water. Set aside and cool.
- In a large bowl, combine cooked quinoa, tomatoes, feta cheese, cucumber, onion, and olives. Stir gently until mixed.
- Stir in lemon pepper and dill.
- Fold in juice of lemon and mix.
- Serve immediately or cover and refrigerate for later.

SERVES 4 FOR LUNCH

NOTE: *This is an easy lunch to make ahead for the week using great fresh summer ingredients. The saltiness of the feta and the briny olives makes this protein-packed vegetarian salad a delicious lunch to make ahead for the week.*

SUMMER PASTA SALAD WITH PESTO SAUCE 

40 ounces cheese tortellini, fresh or frozen

1 cup pesto (store-bought or see recipe for basil pesto on page 137)

½ cup white wine tarragon vinegar

1 pound fresh asparagus, cut diagonally into about 1-inch pieces, then blanched

2 cups red, yellow, and orange bell peppers, thinly sliced

½ cup pecans, chopped

- Cook tortellini according to package instructions.
- Rinse tortellini in cold water, drain, and place in large bowl.
- In a medium bowl, whisk together pesto and vinegar until thoroughly blended.
- Add asparagus, bell peppers, and pecans to the sauce and mix well.
- Pour vegetable mixture over tortellini and toss to coat.
- Cover and store in the refrigerator.

SERVES 10

CORN, BACON, AND TOMATO SALAD 

¼ pound bacon, chopped

½ cup red onion, diced

2 to 3 cups corn, fresh

2 cups grape or cherry tomatoes, halved

1 medium ripe avocado, pitted, peeled, and chopped

½ cup chopped fresh cilantro, more or less

Juice of 1 lime

Salt

- Cook bacon in a skillet over medium-high heat until it begins to render fat.
- Add onion and cook until just softened, about 5 minutes.
- Add corn to skillet, stirring pan occasionally about 5 more minutes.
- Remove from heat, drain fat, and let the corn mixture cool.
- Add tomatoes, avocado, and cilantro.
- Toss with lime juice and salt to taste.

SERVES 6 AS A SIDE

NOTE: *This bright salad is easy to make ahead and bring to a party or it can add some vegetables and color to a grilled chicken dinner.*

CORNBREAD SALAD

2 boxes (8½ ounces) corn muffin mix

3 medium tomatoes, diced

1 bunch green onions, diced

1 green bell pepper, diced

½ to 1 cup bacon bits

1 pint mayonnaise

Ground pepper to taste

- Prepare cornbread according to package directions. Let cool.
- When cool, crumble into pea-sized pieces in a large bowl.
- Mix in tomatoes, green onions, bell pepper, bacon bits (use as many as you like), and mayonnaise. Season with pepper to taste.
- Refrigerate until ready to serve. It's best if it can rest overnight for flavors to blend, but at least 2 hours.

SERVES 8 TO 10 AS A SIDE

NOTE: *At first this recipe may seem odd, but everyone who tries it adds it to their summer menu. A twist on summer salads, this uses cornbread instead of pasta or potatoes as the starch. The sweetness of the cornbread with the crunch of the peppers and bacon bits creates a bright, flavorful side for a summer dinner party.*

NORA'S POTATO SALAD 

SALAD

5 pounds Yukon gold potatoes

1 to 2 green bell peppers, rough-diced

2 to 3 red bell peppers, rough-diced

5 to 6 large celery ribs, chopped

1 Vidalia onion, minced in food processor

3 to 4 hard-boiled eggs, chopped

1 small jar green olives with pimentos, rough-chopped

4 to 5 tablespoons sweet pickle relish

DRESSING

8 ounces mayonnaise

8 to 12 ounces yellow mustard

1 tablespoon Cajun seasoning (or paprika for a milder dressing)

SALAD

- Fill a large pot (at least 8 quarts) with lightly salted water.
- Peel the potatoes and boil to tenderness for approximately 15 minutes.
- When potatoes easily cut with a butter knife, they are done.
- Drain and gently rinse potatoes under cold water, then transfer to a large bowl.
- Mash potatoes with a hand masher to a rough mashed potato consistency.
- Cover with foil or plastic wrap and chill for at least two hours.
- Chop vegetables while potatoes chill.

DRESSING

- In a medium mixing bowl, blend mayonnaise and mustard until the dressing is a medium yellow color. The exact proportion of mustard will vary based on taste.
- Stir in Cajun seasoning (or paprika). Adjust to taste.
- Once potatoes have chilled, stir in vegetables, eggs, olives, relish, and dressing. Serve immediately or return to refrigerator to chill.

SERVES 10 TO 12

NOTE: *This potato salad packs vegetable crunch and a punch, distinguishing it from ordinary potato salad. Mix up the seasoning or type of mustard to create some variety.*

BASIL PESTO 

4 garlic cloves, peeled
2 tablespoons olive oil, divided
1 cup pine nuts
4 to 5 bunches of fresh basil

1 cup of freshly grated Parmesan cheese
Salt to taste

- Preheat oven to 350°F.
- Coat garlic cloves with olive oil and roast in the oven on a cookie sheet for 20 to 30 minutes or until cloves are golden, soft, and fragrant.
- In the same oven, a toaster oven, or a pan on the stove, dry roast (don't add oil) the pine nuts for 3 to 5 minutes until they are golden brown. Be careful not to burn them.
- In a blender or food processor, combine basil leaves, 3 cloves of roasted garlic, ¾ cup toasted pine nuts, ¼ cup Parmesan cheese, and a splash of olive oil.
- Blend until combined, adding olive oil slowly until desired consistency. For thicker pesto, use less olive oil, add more for a thinner sauce.
- Add remaining garlic clove, pine nuts, and remaining cheese.
- Add salt to taste.
- Use pesto with cooked pasta, vegetables, quinoa, or salad.

MAKES ABOUT 1 CUP OF PESTO

ROTINI ITALIAN PASTA SALAD

32 ounces dry tri-color rotini
1 green bell pepper, diced
1 orange bell pepper, diced
1 cup sun-dried tomatoes
(drain if packed in oil)
1 pound thick cut deli ham
1 cup pepperoni slices, halved

1 cup mozzarella cheese,
shredded
1 onion, diced
1 can (2 ounces) sliced black
olives
1 bottle (16 ounces) Italian
dressing

- Cook rotini according to package instructions.
- When done, run rotini under cold water to stop the cooking process.
- In a very large bowl, stir in bell peppers, sun-dried tomatoes, ham, pepperoni, mozzarella cheese, onion, and olives until mixed well. Stir in Italian dressing, using more or less to your liking. Cover and refrigerate at least 3 hours to overnight.

SERVES 16 TO 20

NOTE: *Pasta salad is a summer barbecue staple. Make it gluten-free with rice noodles or dairy-free by skipping the cheese.*

SUMMER VEGETABLE GRILL FOIL PACK

2 medium yellow squash
2 medium zucchini
1 small onion, diced

Olive oil
Salt and pepper to taste

- Place a large piece of foil flat on the counter.
- Slice yellow squash and zucchini into ¼-inch thick rounds.
- Place yellow squash, zucchini, and onion in the center of the foil and fold up all 4 edges to create an open box.
- Drizzle enough olive oil to coat the vegetables.
- Sprinkle with salt and pepper.
- Place the second sheet of foil on top and crimp the edges over the bottom sheet to seal vegetables inside the foil.
- Place on upper rack of a hot grill for 15 minutes or until vegetables are cooked to desired tenderness.

SERVES 4 AS A SIDE

EASY CHICKEN AND VEGETABLE KABOBS 

2 pounds boneless, skinless chicken breasts

1 cup store-bought, fat-free Italian dressing, divided

¾ cup low sodium soy sauce, divided

1 yellow bell pepper, cut into 1-inch pieces

1 red bell pepper, cut into 1-inch pieces

1 large red onion, cut into 1-inch pieces

8 ounces whole button mushrooms

Wooden skewers

- Cube chicken breast into 1 to 2-inch pieces.
- In a large zip top bag, combine chicken, ¾ cup Italian dressing, and ½ cup soy sauce.
- In a second large zip top bag, combine bell peppers, onion, mushrooms, ¼ cup Italian dressing, and ¼ cup soy sauce.
- Refrigerate both bags for at least 4 hours to overnight.
- Build skewers, alternating chicken, pepper, onion, and mushroom.
- Heat grill to medium high heat. Cook skewers about 15 minutes turning halfway through, until chicken is cooked.

SERVES 4

NOTE: *This marinade is an easy shortcut full of flavor without a lot of work. Serve with cooked rice or with a side of Jalapeño Ranch Dip (page 126). To prevent the wooden skewers from burning on the grill, soak in water for 1 hour prior to using.*

YELLOW SQUASH CASSEROLE 

4 cups sliced yellow squash
½ large onion, chopped
35 butter crackers, crushed
1 cup shredded Cheddar cheese
2 eggs, beaten

¾ cup milk
½ cup butter, melted
1 teaspoon salt
Ground black pepper to taste
2 tablespoons butter

- Preheat oven to 400°F.
- Place squash and onion in a large skillet over medium heat.
- Pour in a small amount of water. Cover, and cook until squash is tender, for about 5 minutes.
- Drain well, and place in a large bowl.
- In a medium bowl, mix together cracker crumbs and cheese.
- Stir half of cracker mixture into the cooked squash and onions.
- In a small bowl, mix together eggs and milk. Add to squash mixture.
- Stir in ¼ cup melted butter and season with salt and pepper.
- Spread into a 9 x 13-inch baking dish.
- Sprinkle with remaining cracker mixture and dot with 2 tablespoons butter.
- Bake in preheated oven for 25 minutes or until lightly browned.

SERVES 10 TO 12 AS A SIDE

WINE TOUR QUINOA

2 cups quinoa, uncooked
⅓ cup olive oil
1 teaspoon seasoned salt, or to taste

¼ cup fresh chives, finely chopped
½ cup almonds, chopped
½ cup dried apricots, chopped
1 lemon, zested and juiced

- Cook quinoa according to package directions.
- Move to medium bowl and cool.
- Add olive oil, salt, chives, almonds, and apricots.
- Stir thoroughly to combine.
- Gently stir in lemon juice and lemon zest.
- Refrigerate for several hours or overnight before serving.

SERVES 8 TO 10 AS A SIDE

NOTE: *An easy make ahead recipe, this quinoa dish is great for lunch or served with a grilled fish dinner.*

CHICKEN SAUTÉED WITH WINE AND MUSHROOMS

1 tablespoon olive oil
½ Vidalia onion, diced
8 ounces baby bella mushrooms
1 tablespoon Italian seasoning

¾ pound boneless, skinless chicken breasts
¼ cup dry white wine
Salt and pepper to taste

- Heat olive oil in a large skillet over medium high heat.
- Sauté onion and mushroom with seasoning until onions are almost clear.
- Add chicken and begin to brown.
- Add white wine, reduce to low heat, and cook until wine is absorbed.

SERVES 2

NOTE: *This is a simple and flavorful weeknight dinner for two, but it is easy to double if you're cooking for more people. Serve on rice or quinoa or with a side of green vegetables.*

MACADAMIA NUT-CRUSTED MAHI MAHI

6 tablespoons macadamia nuts
½ cup plain bread crumbs
1 egg plus 1 egg white
6 (6 ounce) mahi mahi fillets
½ cup butter
¼ cup shallots, diced
4 cups chicken stock

½ cup pineapple, chopped
½ cup papaya, chopped
½ cup mango, chopped
2 tablespoons shredded coconut
1 tablespoon red pepper flakes
Salt and pepper to taste
Sugar to taste

- Preheat oven to 350°F.
- In a food processor, pulse together nuts and bread crumbs until finely ground.
- Pour nut mixture onto plate.
- In a separate dish, beat egg and egg white.
- Dip fish fillets in egg, then coat on both sides with bread crumb mixture.
- Heat butter in large skillet over medium heat. Fry fillets on both sides until golden brown. Remove and transfer to baking pan.
- Add shallots to skillet and cook until translucent.
- Stir in chicken stock.
- Mix in pineapple, papaya, mango, coconut, and red pepper flakes.
- Season with salt, pepper, and sugar to taste.
- Simmer mixture until sauce is thick (about 30 minutes). Reserve in pan over low heat.
- Bake mahi mahi in preheated oven, about 10 minutes, until internal temperature is 140°F. Remove fish and lightly coat with sauce.

SERVES 6

NOTE: *If you're looking to use tropical fruit for something other than a snack or a salsa, this recipe is it. This dish will transport you to warm breezes and waving palm trees. A fantastic combination of bold flavors and light fish, this also works well with chicken and pairs well with our Tropical Salad and Pineapple Vinaigrette [page 128].*

BAKED SPEDINI SKEWERS

1 pound boneless, skinless chicken breasts

2 cups seasoned Italian breadcrumbs

½ cup grated Parmesan cheese

1 teaspoon basil (fresh or dried)

1 teaspoon oregano (fresh or dried)

3 garlic cloves, minced

2 eggs

Sliced Parmesan cheese (optional)

1 large onion, cut into 1-inch squares

1 large green pepper, cut into 1-inch squares

1 large red pepper, cut into 1-inch squares

5 to 6 bay leaves

Salt and pepper to taste

1 can (15 ounces) seasoned diced tomatoes (may substitute 2 large, diced fresh tomatoes)

- Preheat oven to 375°F.
- Wrap chicken breasts in plastic wrap and pound until thin and tender.
- Cut into strips approximately 1-inch wide by 3 to 4-inches long.
- Mix bread crumbs with Parmesan, basil, oregano, and garlic, and set aside.
- Beat eggs in a separate bowl.
- Dredge chicken in beaten egg and then coat in bread crumbs.
- Roll chicken into spirals. Insert small piece of sliced Parmesan in center if desired.
- Skewer chicken, and alternate chicken, onion, and peppers on each skewer.
- Include one bay leaf per 1 to 2 skewers. Each skewer should hold 3 to 4 chicken spirals.
- Coat 9 x 13-inch pan with cooking spray. Place skewers in pan, adding and salt pepper to taste.
- Bake in preheated oven for 35 to 40 minutes or until chicken is cooked through.
- Add diced tomatoes for last 10 minutes of cooking.

SERVES 4

NOTE: *These skewers are loaded with Italian flavor, and especially great if you don't have a grill or the weather is unfavorable. Feel free to add more Parmesan or melt mozzarella cheese on top of the tomatoes during the last 10 minutes of cooking. And don't forget to remove the bay leaves before eating!*

PULLED PORK 

2 bay leaves, crushed

1¼ teaspoons cardamom

2 teaspoons coriander

1 teaspoon cumin

2½ teaspoons ground fennel

1 tablespoon paprika

1 tablespoon coarse salt

2 teaspoons black pepper

¼ cup extra virgin olive oil

5 garlic cloves, minced into a paste

2 tablespoons brown sugar

3 pound pork shoulder, skin on

- In a small bowl, combine bay leaves, spices, salt, pepper, olive oil, garlic, and sugar.

- Score skin of pork shoulder with a sharp knife.

- Rub paste evenly on meat. Cover tightly with cling wrap and let rest in fridge for at least 3 hours or overnight.

- Preheat oven to 450°F.

- In a large roasting pan, roast pork uncovered for 30 minutes.

- Cover with foil and turn oven down to 300°F.

- Bake for 3 hours. For a larger piece of pork, add 1 additional hour per pound.

SERVES 6

NOTE: *This pulled pork recipe is great for any occasion. Serve it up on sandwiches, as a plate with cold salads, or even eat it for breakfast with a fried egg on top. The rub is substantial, so it is easy to increase the size of the pork shoulder to serve more people. It can also be made in a slow cooker; cook on low for 8 hours for a 3 to 4-pound shoulder.*

BABY BACK RIBS

Olive oil spray
¼ cup brown sugar
1½ tablespoons paprika
1 tablespoon kosher salt
1½ tablespoons pepper

1 teaspoon garlic powder
1 teaspoon onion powder
¼ to ½ teaspoon cayenne pepper
3 racks baby back ribs
Favorite barbecue sauce

- Fold heavy duty foil in half, making sure to use a piece big enough to fold in half and still hold a rack of ribs.
- Coat heavy duty foil with olive oil spray.
- Place a rack of ribs on a doubled-over piece of foil.
- In a small bowl, combine brown sugar, paprika, salt, pepper, garlic powder, onion powder, and cayenne pepper. Mix well.
- Rub each rack of ribs with dry rub.
- Cover each rack with two pieces of foil and crimp all edges together tightly.
- Let ribs sit in the fridge for at least 3 hours to overnight.
- When ready to cook, bake at 300°F for 2 to 2½ hours on a rimmed baking sheet.
- Remove foil and brush ribs with barbecue sauce on both sides.
- Broil for 5 minutes on each side.

SERVES 6

NOTE: *These simple ribs are always a treat. Cooked low and slow, they are great for a summer dinner party or any time of year.*

OLD-FASHIONED CUSTARD PIE 

4 eggs
¾ cup sugar
2 cups 2 percent milk
(1¾ cups if using skim)

1 teaspoon vanilla extract
¼ cup butter
Nutmeg to taste
Single pie crust (optional)

- Preheat oven to 400°F.
- Place eggs, sugar, milk, and vanilla in blender and blend for 3 minutes.
- If using pie crust, place single crust in 9-inch pie plate and crimp edges.
- If not using crust, use a glass 8 or 9-inch pie plate.
- Pour filling into crust/pie plate. Sprinkle nutmeg over unbaked pie.
- Bake for 40 to 45 minutes until pie filling is firm.

SERVES 8

NOTE: *This custard pie is quick to make and always wows guests with its bold flavor. Make it gluten-free by skipping the crust or even using a gluten-free crust. Serve with vanilla bean ice cream or top with fresh berries.*

FOURTH OF JULY BERRY TRIFLE 

1 premade angel food cake
1 container (8 ounces) frozen whipped topping, thawed

1 pound fresh strawberries, hulled and sliced
1 pound fresh blueberries

- Cut angel food cake into bite-size pieces.
- Place a layer of cake across the bottom of the trifle dish.
- Add a layer of whipped topping, followed by a layer of strawberries and blueberries. Repeat until you reach the top of the trifle dish.
- Finish the trifle with one last layer of whipped topping. Decorate the top with a pattern of blueberries and strawberries (flag, star, border).
- Store in the fridge until ready to serve.

SERVES 8 TO 10

NOTE: *This festive dish can be assembled in no time. Because the cake will get soggy if it is made ahead, it is best to make and serve the day of your event.*

RED, WHITE, AND BLUE BUNDT CAKE

CAKE

2½ cups plus 3 tablespoons all-purpose flour

2 teaspoons baking powder

1 teaspoon salt

1 cup unsalted butter, room temperature

1¾ cups granulated sugar

Zest of 1 lemon

2 teaspoons vanilla extract

3 large eggs

¾ cup buttermilk

1 pint blueberries

1 pint strawberries

GLAZE

Juice of 1 lemon

2 cups powdered sugar

CAKE

- Preheat oven to 350°F.
- Spray a 10-cup Bundt cake pan with nonstick spray.
- In a large bowl, sift together 2½ cups of flour, baking powder, and salt.
- In a stand mixer or large bowl with electric mixer, beat together butter, sugar, lemon zest, and vanilla on medium speed until fluffy.
- Beat in eggs one at a time.
- Add flour mixture and buttermilk, alternating until combined. Continue mixing on medium. The batter will be very thick.
- In a separate bowl, mix 3 tablespoons of flour with berries until coated.
- Fold berries into cake batter.
- Spread batter in prepared Bundt cake pan.
- Bake for 50 to 60 minutes until a knife comes out clean.
- Cool completely on a wire rack before flipping out of pan.

GLAZE

- Combine lemon juice and powdered sugar in a bowl.
- Whisk until thick.
- Add more lemon juice or melted butter if you like a thinner consistency.
- Top cake with glaze when it is completely cool.

SERVES 10 TO 12

NOTE: *This Bundt cake is always a hit during the summer. Add or swap with other berries (like blackberries) to your liking. A great party dessert, this cake is also a favorite for a sweet summer breakfast.*

NO-BAKE HEAVENLY PIE 

8 ounces cream cheese, room temperature

1 can (14 ounces) sweetened condensed milk

⅓ cup fresh lemon juice

1 container (8 ounces) frozen whipped topping, thawed

½ cup pecans, chopped

1 cup canned crushed pineapple, drained (can also use fresh, cut into small chunks)

2 (9-inch) graham cracker pie shells

- In a large mixing bowl, combine cream cheese, milk, and lemon juice.
- Beat with a hand mixer until smooth.
- Fold in whipped topping until just combined.
- Stir in pecans and pineapple. Mix well.
- Divide batter evenly, pouring into 2 pie shells.
- Refrigerate for at least 3 hours before serving.

MAKES 2 PIES. EACH PIE SERVES 8.

NOTE: *If you want to make a sweet dessert without heating up the oven in the summer, this pie comes together in the refrigerator. It also freezes well so you can eat one now and save one for later.*

TABBERT'S BRANDY SLUSH 

SIMPLE SYRUP

7 cups water

2 cups sugar

TEA

2 cups water

4 black tea bags

MIX

12 ounces lemonade concentrate

2 ounces brandy

12 ounces orange juice concentrate

- Bring 7 cups water and 2 cups sugar to a boil to create a simple syrup. Cool.
- Steep 4 black tea bags in 2 cups boiling water for 10 minutes. Cool.
- Combine simple syrup, tea, concentrates, and brandy in a freezable container.
- Freeze until the mixture is the desired consistency, about 3 hours.

MAKES 1 LARGE PITCHER

HAWAIIAN BANANA NUT BREAD 

**3 cups all-purpose flour
(substitute 2 cups white flour
and 1 cup whole wheat flour)**

2 cups sugar

1 teaspoon baking soda

1 teaspoon salt

1 teaspoon cinnamon

**1 cup chopped pecans
(can omit if desired)**

3 eggs, beaten

1½ cups vegetable oil

2 cups mashed bananas

**1 can (8 ounces) crushed
pineapple, drained**

2 teaspoons vanilla extract

- Preheat oven to 350°F.
- Grease and lightly flour two 9 x 5 x 3-inch loaf pans.
- In a large mixing bowl, combine flour, sugar, baking soda, salt, cinnamon, and nuts. Set aside.
- In a medium bowl, combine eggs, oil, bananas, pineapple, and vanilla.
- Add wet ingredients to dry ingredients, stirring until moistened.
- Bake in preheated oven for 60 to 65 minutes, or until done (toothpick inserted should come out clean).
- Cool 10 minutes before removing to wire rack to cool completely.

MAKES 2 LOAVES OF BREAD

NOTE: *A twist on regular banana nut bread, pineapple adds some summer flavor. This recipe is a great way to use up overripe bananas in your kitchen and freezes well.*

ICE CREAM TORTE

1 package (16 ounces) chocolate sandwich cookies

¾ stick butter or margarine, melted

½ gallon vanilla ice cream (preferably in a square), softened

1 jar (12 ounces) fudge topping, slightly warmed

1 container (16 ounces) frozen whipped topping, thawed

- Crush up cookies by hand or process in a food processor.
- In a bowl, combine melted butter and cookies.
- Press mixture evenly into the bottom of an 8 x 12-inch baking pan.
- Cut ice cream into slabs and place on top of cookie mixture.
- Warm fudge topping in microwave and spread over ice cream.
- Spread whipped topping across ice cream.
- Place pan in freezer to set, about 2 hours. Remove 15 minutes before serving.

SERVES 10 TO 12

NOTE: *Use fresh berries, nuts, or sprinkles to top the torte.*

NOTES

152

NOTES

NOTES

2015-2016 COOKBOOK COMMITTEE

CHAIR

Allyson Funk Baker

MEMBERS

Gabrielle Durand	Gretchyn Meinken
Leah Hapner	SallyJean Penna
Jeri Kirschner	Kristie Pichler
Erica McCants	Kristin Westover

2016-2017 COOKBOOK COMMITTEE

CHAIR

Leah Hapner

MEMBERS

Allyson Funk Baker	Renee Rothschild
Marissa Lawson	Ashely Soldan
Erica McCants	Jen Van Trump
Jenna Parkhurst	Maggie Weatherly

2017-2018 COOKBOOK COMMITTEE

CHAIR

Marissa Lawson

MEMBERS

Jessica Brown	Lauren Killick
Julie Bryant	Molly Marcheski
Heather Carroll	Renee Rothschild
Katherine Jenezon	Jessica Walters Sabino

RECIPE CONTRIBUTORS

Sarah Baker

Allyson Funk Baker

Kimberly Beach

Jennifer Bell

Julie Bonifay

Denise Booth

Allie Bosak

Doris Brown

Anna Bryant

Brianne Burnett Powers

Michelle Cogan

Kelly Cruz

Nima Patel Edwards

Kelli Edwards

Alyscia Eisen

Katie Eubank

Monika Geraci

Mary Glodoski

Stephany Smith-Hafezi

Leah Hapner

Jennifer Herrin

Allie Hummel

Sarah Lantz

Tanina Linden

Paula MacDonald

Tara McCook

Gretchyn Meinken

Anita Molina

J.J. Newby Ketzle

Robin Nicholas

Maria Posey

Amy Prewett

Lauren Pulford

Elizabeth Ross

Katherine Scott

Caroline Simms

Jennifer Smith

Hayley Smith

Cheryl Tabbert

Lori Ann Terjesen

Lynsey Wallace

Maggie Weatherly

Kimberly Weisenberger

Kristin Westover

Kate Zawacki

RECIPE TESTERS

Stephanie Andrejcak

Allyson Funk Baker

Kimberly Beach

Taylor Bezerra

Katie Brock

Kelli Crawford

Gabrielle Durand

Eileen Foyle

Leah Hapner

Sharon Johnsen

Michele Kinsella

Jeri Kirschner

Jessica Markey

Erica McCants

Gretchyn Meinken

Stephanie Morgano

Melody Peppard

Lara Ramsey

Jennifer Nelson Saracevic

Caroline Simms

Hayley Smith

Jessica Walters Sabino

Mary Weatherly

Kim Weisenberger

Katherine Werther

Kristin Westover

EDITING AND CODING CONTRIBUTORS

Monica Alford

Michaela Barrett

Heather Browning

Kelly Cruz

Colleen Geasey

Aleese Hopkins

Jessica Markey

Danielle Muenzfeld

Anna Perry

Paige Ruddy

Monique Rush

Crystal Riley

Celeste Roney

Jennifer Saracevic

Nicole Semenza

Devon Snodgrass

JUNIOR LEAGUE OF NORTHERN VIRGINIA
2014-2015 BOARD OF DIRECTORS

Whitney Richardson, *President*

Beatriz Duque Long, *President-Elect*

Kelly Cruz, *Secretary*

Kimberly Beach, *Parliamentarian*

Lisa Flach-Fulcher, *Treasurer*

Gretchen Ehle, *Treasurer-Elect*

Ali Patty, *Communications Council Director*

Alyia Gaskins, *Community Council Director*

Stephany Smith, *Fund Development Council Director*

Robin Robinson, *Membership Council Director*

Kristie Pichler, *Planning Council Director*

Joan Irey, *Sustainer Representative*

Susan Joyce, *Sustainer Representative*

Jenn Williston, *Nominating and Placements Chair*

Elizabeth Ross, *Nominating and Placements Chair-Elect*

Shashuana Littlejohn, *Assistant to the President*

2015-2016 BOARD OF DIRECTORS

Beatriz Duque Long, *President*

Lori Ann Terjesen, Ph.D., *President-Elect*

Sharon Ballard, *Secretary*

Kelly Atkinson, *Parliamentarian*

Gretchen Ehle, *Treasurer*

Stephany Smith-Hafezi, *Treasurer-Elect*

Martha Hess, *Communications Council Director*

Celia Anderson, *Community Council Director*

Kelly Cruz, *Fund Development Council Director*

Jennifer Bell, *Membership Council Director*

Kimberly Beach, *Planning Council Director*

Alissa Redding, *Sustainer Representative*

Elizabeth Ross, *Nominating and Placements Chair*

Brianne Powers, *Nominating and Placements Chair-Elect*

Anita Molina, *Assistant to the President*

2016-2017 BOARD OF DIRECTORS

Lori Ann Terjesen, Ph.D., *President*

Martha Hess, *President-Elect*

Sharon Ballard, *Secretary*

Jennifer Williston, *Parliamentarian*

Stephany Smith-Hafezi, *Treasurer*

Lourdes Garcia-Calderon, *Treasurer-Elect*

LaShaunda Ford, *Communications Council Director*

Celia Anderson, *Community Council Director*

Krysta Jones, *Fund Development Director*

Anna Bryant, *Membership Council Director*

Jazmen Jackson, *Planning Council Director*

Tamara Baptiste, *Sustainer Representative*

Brianne Powers, *Nominating and Placements Chair*

Monika Geraci, *Nominating and Placements Chair-Elect*

Paula MacDonald, *Assistant to the President*

2017-2018 BOARD OF DIRECTORS

Martha Hess, *President*

Celia Anderson, *President-Elect*

Betsy Swift Porter, *Secretary*

Tarren Smarr, *Parliamentarian*

Lourdes Garcia-Calderon, *Treasurer*

Alyscia Eisen, *Treasurer-Elect*

Anna Bryant, *Communications Council Director*

Hayley Smith, *Community Council Director*

Krysta Jones, *Fund Development Director*

Lauren Crowder, *Membership Council Director*

Sashuana Littlejohn, *Planning Council Director*

Nicki Crane, *Sustainer Representative*

Monika Geraci, *Nominating and Placements Chair*

Sharon Ballard, *Nominating and Placements Chair-Elect*

Kimberly Beach, *Assistant to the President*

A

B

GRILLING RECIPES

GRITS *(see Cereals and Grains)*

K

L

LEMON

INDEX

INDEX

INDEX

CONVERSION OF PAN AND UTENSIL SIZES

UTENSIL	Measure (Volume)	Measure (Cm)	Measure (Inches)
Baking or cake pan	2 L	20 cm square	8-inch square
	2.5 L	23 cm square	9-inch square
	3 L	30 x 20 x 5	12 x 8 x 2
	3.5 L	33 x 21 x 5	13 x 9 x 2
Cookie sheet		40 x 30	16 x 12
Jelly-roll pan	2 L	40 x 25 x 2	15 x 10 x ¾
Loaf pan	1.5 L	20 x 10 x 7	8 x 4 x 3
	2 L	23 x 13 x 7	9 x 5 x 3
Round layer cake pan	1.2 L	20 x 4	8 x 1½
			9 x 1½
Pie pan	750 ml	20 x 3	8 x 1¼
	1 L	23 x 3	9 x 1¼
Tube pan	2 L	20 x 7	8 x 3
	3 L	23 x 10	9 x 4
Springform pan	2.5 L	23 x 6	9 x 3
	3 L	25 x 8	10 x 4
Baking dish	1 L		1 quart
	1.5 L		1½ quart
	2 L		2 quart
	2.5 L		2½ quart
	3 L		3 quart
	4 L		4 quart
Custard cup	200 ml		6 fl. oz.
Muffin pans	40 ml	4 x 2.5	1½ x 1
	75 ml	5 x 3.5	2 x 1¼
	100 ml	7.5 x 3.5	3 x 1½
Mixing bowls	1 L		1 quart
	2 L		2 quart
	3 L		3 quarts

EQUIVALENTS AND SUBSTITUTIONS

1 pound shelled walnuts	3 cups chopped walnuts
1 pound raisins	2¾ cups seedless raisins
1 pound dates	2½ cups pitted dates
1 tablespoon cornstarch	2 tablespoons flour or 4 teaspoons tapioca
1 medium garlic clove	⅛ teaspoon garlic powder
1 cup honey	1 cup molasses or corn syrup
1 cup ketchup	1 cup tomato sauce plus ½ cup sugar plus 2 tablespoons vinegar
1 teaspoon dry mustard	1 tablespoon prepared mustard
1 small onion	1 tablespoon dried onion
1 cup tomato juice	½ cup tomato sauce plus ½ cup water
1 cup self-rising flour	1 cup flour plus 1½ tablespoons baking powder plus ½ teaspoon salt
1 cup corn syrup	1 cup sugar plus ¼ cup liquid
1 cup buttermilk/sour milk	1 tablespoon lemon juice plus enough milk to equal 1 cup. Let stand for 5 minutes.
1 cup sour cream	1 cup plain yogurt
1 cup tomato juice	½ cup tomato paste plus ½ cup water

VEGETABLE TIMETABLE — MINUTES

VEGETABLE	Boiled	Steamed	Baked
Asparagus	10-15		
Asparagus, tied in bundles	20-30		
Artichokes, French	40	45-60	
Bean, Lima	20	30	
Bean, Green	10-15	20	
Beets, young with skins on	30	60	70-90
Beets, old	60-120	60-120	
Broccoli, florets	5-10		
Broccoli, stems	20-30		
Brussels Sprouts	20-30		
Cabbage, chopped	10-20	25	
Cauliflower, stem down	20-30		
Cauliflower, florets	8-10		
Carrots, cut across	20-30	40	
Chard	60-90	90	
Celery, 1½ inch pieces	20-30	45	
Corn, green, tender	5-10	15	
Corn on the cob	8-10	15	
Eggplant, whole	30	40	45
Marrow	15-40		
Onions	25-40	60	60-75
Parsnips	25-40	60	60-75
Peas	5-15	5-15	
Peppers	20-30	30	30
Potatoes, depending on size	20-40	60	45-60
Potatoes, sweet	40	40	45-60
Scalloped potatoes			60-90
Pumpkin, in cubes	30	45	60
Tomatoes, depending on size	5-15	50	15-20
Turnips, depending on size	25-40		

SAUCES

WHITE SAUCE	Liquid	Thickening	Fat	Salt
No. 1 thin	1 cup milk	1 T flour	1 T	½ t
No. 2 medium	1 cup milk	2 T flour	1½ T	1½ t
No. 3 med-thick	1 cup milk	3 T flour	2 T	1 t
No. 4 thick	1 cup milk	4 T flour	2½ T	1 t

Use No. 1 sauce for cream soups.
Use No. 2 sauce for creamed or scalloped dishes or gravy.
Use No. 3 sauce for soufflés.
Use No. 4 sauce for croquettes.

HEALTHY FOOD SUBSTITUTIONS

INSTEAD OF THIS		TRY THIS	
Original Item	**Calories**	**Healthier Choice**	**Calories**
1 cup mashed potatoes	100	Mashed cauliflower	100
1 cup sour cream	480	1 cup Greek yogurt	140
3 slices pork bacon	130	3 slices turkey bacon	108
½ cup vegetable oil (baking)	960	½ cup applesauce	50
1 cup 2% milk	120	1 cup unsweetened almond milk	40
1 cup cooked pasta	220	1 cup cooked whole wheat pasta	175
1 small flour tortilla	95	1 small corn tortilla	52
1 tablespoon butter (sautéing)	200	1 second cooking spray	8
3 oz chicken thigh with skin	200	3 oz chicken thigh without skin	165
1 pound regular ground beef	1,200	1 pound extra lean ground beef	680